Woodwork for Winemakers

By
C. J. DART
and
D. A. SMITH

How to construct simply and cheaply items of equipment to render your winemaking and brewing easier and more efficient. Many items described in this book cannot be purchased, but can be easily made from wood by anyone with a limited knowledge of carpentry.

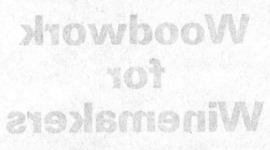

First Impression: March 1971
Second Impression: August 1971
Third Impression: February 1972
Fourth Impression: February 1973
Fifth Impression: March 1975
Sixth Impression: December 1976
Seventh Impression: February 1978

SBN 0 900841 17 6

Printed in Great Britain by:
Standard Press (Andover) Ltd., Andover, Hants.
Telephone: 2413

Contents

CHAPTER		PAGE
1	**MATERIALS AND METHODS**	6
2	**PREPARATION**	
	Fruit pulper	9
	Hand Fruit Crusher	16
	Club Size Press and Stand	18
	Small Press	25
	Simple Weighing Balance	29
3	**FERMENTATION**	
	Large and Small Stirrers	31
	Plonker/Sinker	32
	Pulp Squeezer	34
	8 Jar Cupboard	36
	Fermentation Cupboard. Electrics Diagram	40
	4 Jar Cupboard	41
	6 Jar Cupboard (External)	41
	Bin or Carboy Trolley	45
4	**AFTER FERMENTATION**	
	Floating Syphon	46
	Racking and Straining Stand	47
	Bottle Draining Stand	51
	Bottle Corking Holder	53
	Cork Flogger	54
	Labelling and Filling Gauge	55
5	**STORING AND SERVING**	
	Bottle Rack. Type 1	57
	Bottle Rack. Type 2	59
	Bottle Rack. Type 3	62
	Bottle Rack for Sideboard	66
	½ Gallon Jar Dispenser	69
	1 Gallon Jar Dispenser	73
	Mobile Bar	75

6   **SHED WINERY**

     The Site, Base, Insulation
     Electricity, Work Bench and Layout   80

7   **MISCELLANEOUS**

     Small Items Cupboard   95
     Winemaker's Cupboard   98
     Record Card Index Box   101
     Bottle Carrier   103
     Malt Grain Crusher   105
     Shelves and Patent Shelving   108

8   **YOUNG WINEMAKER**

     Dad's Apron   114
     Beer Mats   114
     Bottle Waistcoat   116
     Straining and Press Bags   116

Photographs

Fruit Pulper   Plate 1
Club Size Press   Plate 2
Small Press   Plate 3
Straining Stand   Plate 3
Pulp Squeezer   Plate 4
Useful Equipment   Plate 4
Bottle Racks   Plate 5
Bottle Draining Stand   Plate 6
8 Jar Fermentation Cupboard   Plate 6
Small Items Cabinet   Plate 7
½ Gallon Jar Dispenser   Plate 7
Bottle Carrier   **Plate 8**
Malt Grain Crusher   **Plate 8**

Preface

In writing this book on equipment that can be easily constructed by the home wine maker, we had to give a lot of thought to the choice of materials. As the principal material we have settled on wood, owing to its comparative ease of working, be it blockboard, plywood, ordinary softwood, or hardwood, but obviously metal has had to be used in parts of the construction, where wood is just not suitable. A cutting list in imperial and metric measurements is given in the text, together with the recommended materials to use; all have been tested and found suitable for the job required.

Throughout the book great thought has been given to the cost of the finished article; where an expensive material has been suggested it will be found to give the best results, and we have worked on the basis of "minimum best", i.e. the best quality for minimum cost.

We have assumed, of course, that the reader is handy with wood and has a few tools, such as a coping or pad saw for cutting curves, a tenon saw for plywood, and perhaps a handsaw for the larger timbers. Wood can be shaped and finished by plane, rasp, spokeshave or glass-paper. A brace and a small selection of drill bits are needed for boring holes when dowelling. (Hardwood dowel is considered more suitable for joining wood than nails or screws, which may rust and contaminate the brew.) An electric drill/sawbench can make much of the work less laborious, and a workbench is desirable but by no means essential; we used the kitchen table for much of our work!

Various manufacturers' products have been mentioned in the text and we thank Mr. H. Ellaway and the several technical departments concerned for their help and, in some cases, patience when we asked so many questions. A list of suppliers is given in the appendices but we have no financial interest in or any connection with, any manufacturer mentioned.

May you get as much enjoyment out of making and using the items of equipment as we had in designing, altering, and perfecting them in the light of experience and use.

CHAPTER 1

Materials and Methods

DOWELLING

Dowel is supplied by most Do-It-Yourself shops, etc., and is obtainable in soft and hardwood. We recommend hardwood dowelling for the construction of articles in this book; it can be purchased in various diameters and lengths to suit the job in hand.

After it is cut to the required length one end is rounded and a groove is cut along its length to prevent glue and air being trapped when the dowel is driven into the prepared hole. To prepare the hole for dowelling, allow a small quantity of glue to run down the side of the hole, coat the rounded end of the dowel with glue, and drive in. Always apply glue to the meeting surfaces before driving in the dowels.

GLUES

Most modern glues, for example, "Unibond", "Resin W.", "Polystik", can be used for nearly all the wood gluing operations as they give an extremely strong and waterproof joint. Other joints will require 'Araldite' or similar adhesive. Surplus glue should always be wiped off with a damp cloth before it hardens otherwise it will be difficult to remove. Remember to use the glue in accordance with the manufacturer's instructions.

GLUE AND PIN

This is an easy and strong method of butt joining two pieces of wood, i.e. thin plywood or stripwood. Veneer or panel pins should be in length approximately three times the thickness of the material being fixed; this is a good guide to the size of pin needed. Apply the glue to the surfaces to be joined, drive in the pins and punch the heads just below the surface and leave to set.

GLUE AND SCREW

As for glue and pin, but is often used for thicker timbers where more strength is required. Pilot holes should be bored and countersunk before driving the screw home.

TIMBER

When purchasing prepared timber its section will be reduced by $\frac{3}{32}$ of an inch for each of the planed sides and edges, e.g. 1″ by 2″ prepared will finish at $\frac{13}{16}$ in. by $1\frac{13}{16}$″. This does not necessarily apply to manufactured materials such as plywood, blockboard, chipboard, etc.

PLYWOOD

This can be purchased from any timber merchant in various thicknesses, often cut to the size required. *It is essential that waterproof or exterior quality plywood is used where the article comes in contact with liquids, as in the bottle draining stand, wine press, or pulp squeezer.* We found that birch ply gave a superior finish to the items and is to be preferred to some of the cheaper, coarse grades.

BLOCKBOARD

This consists of softwood strips glued together between veneers, plywood or hardboard. Care must be exercised when purchasing to ensure that core slats run the length of the larger dimensions. Readily takes nailing, screwing, or dowelling. Like plywood, it is obtainable in various thicknesses.

"CONTIBOARD"

Trade name of Arronson Bros. for chipboard. It is obtainable from D.I.Y. shops in one thickness, various widths and two lengths. It has a veneered finish on two faces and the long edges. Suitable fixings are glue and dowel, or screws. It is ideally suited to items for use in the living room, e.g. fermentation cupboard, mobile bar.

SOFTWOOD

All softwood should be carefully inspected to make sure it is free of shakes, knots, and warp. It is readily available in an infinite variety of sizes.

HARDWOOD

To get the required size and quality this may have to be ordered through your timber merchant. The hardwoods recommended in this book are oak or beech, while for handles ash is often preferred.

METAL

Before drilling metal always mark the centre of the hole to be drilled with a centre punch to prevent the bit skidding on the surface.

PLUGGING BRICKWORK

It is important when fixing cabinets, racks, shelves, etc., to a wall that the hole for the plug should be drilled into the brickwork at least 1½″ deep. The length of the fixing screw must be long enough to pass through the plaster and bite at least 1½″ into the plug in the wall. With a potential weight of hundreds of pounds being loaded on the shelves we do not recommend the use of hardened steel nails for fixing in lieu of plugging brickwork.

GALLON JAR

All measurements relating to a gallon jar are for a standard two ring handle, glass 1 gallon jar or demijohn. If you ferment or store wine in containers other than these, allowance for size should be made accordingly.

FINISHING AND PAINTING

To get a superior finish all surfaces should be rubbed down with a coarse grade and then a fine grade of glass paper. Fill holes with plastic wood coloured to match the veneers where a clear finish is desired. If the article is to be painted the holes may be filled with putty. Where a clear finish is required apply three coats of "Crown" polyurethane varnish, and where gloss paint finish is required, treat knots with shellac knotting, apply one coat of "Crown" acrylic primer/sealer/ undercoat and finish with two coats of "Crown-Plus-Two" polyurethane gloss paint. In both cases the painted work should be allowed to stand, preferably for seven days, to enable the paint systems to harden. These recommendations by the "Walpamur Company" have been found to be most satisfactory.

"Hit and Miss" Ventilators: a trade term for small, sliding, manually-operated ventilators.

Fruit Pulper

We have all at some time laboriously prepared ten or twenty pounds of apples to make a gallon of wine using an ordinary mincer. Even if you intend using a press the fruit must first be pulped. Why not simplify this by making this simple-to-construct pulper? This pulper easily reduces apples to a slurry at an approximate rate of $1\frac{1}{2}$ lb. of fruit per minute. Some such machine is an essential for all winemakers and on test, 84 lb. of mixed apples were pulped and pressed (using the club size press described later) in less than an hour. It is important that all dimensions are strictly observed and good quality oak, beech or waterproof plywood is used in the construction.

CONSTRUCTION

First decide which type of roller is to be used. If a lathe is available, roller type 1 can be quickly made. An alternative roller (type 2), is built up from plywood discs cut to shape with a coping saw.

Turned Roller (type 1)

Glue the four $3'' \times 2''$ pieces together around the $1''$ core as shown in Fig. 1. Take care that no adhesive comes in contact with the core as it is removed after turning. Turn on the lathe until it is $3\frac{5}{8}''$ diameter. Alternatively, you may be able to find a wooden roller of the right diameter (a section of a tent or flagpole?) which can be drilled and then have the hole chiselled square. Or a timber company will prepare one for you. Mark out the positions for the roller teeth and drill the 48 $\frac{7}{32}''$ diameter holes $\frac{1}{2}''$ deep. Mix a small quantity of Araldite and dip the end of each tooth into the adhesive before driving it into the hole. Leave the teeth protruding $\frac{3}{16}''$. Follow Araldite manufacturer's instructions on hardening.

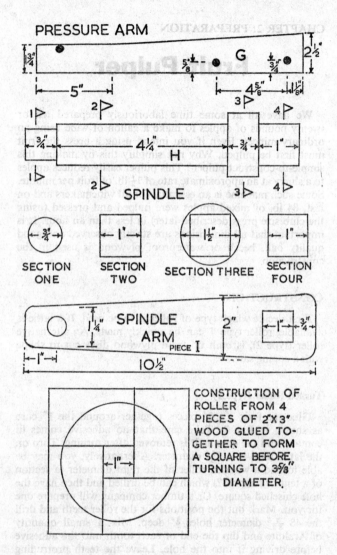

PRESSURE ARM

SPINDLE

SECTION ONE

SECTION TWO

SECTION THREE

SECTION FOUR

SPINDLE ARM PIECE I

CONSTRUCTION OF ROLLER FROM 4 PIECES OF 2"X3" WOOD GLUED TOGETHER TO FORM A SQUARE BEFORE TURNING TO 3⅝" DIAMETER.

Fig. 1

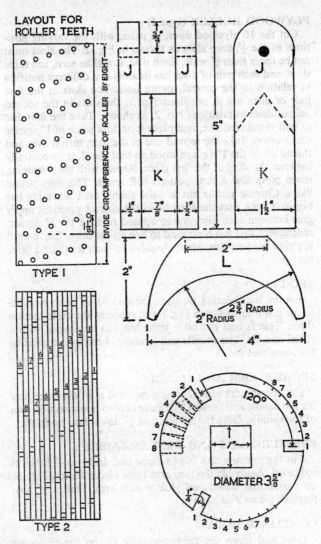

LAYOUT FOR
ROLLER TEETH

TYPE 1

DIVIDE CIRCUMFERENCE OF ROLLER BY EIGHT

$\frac{3}{4}''$

J   J   J

5"

$\frac{1}{2}''$ $\frac{7}{8}''$ $\frac{1}{2}''$

K   K

$1\frac{1}{2}''$

2"

L

2" RADIUS

$2\frac{3}{4}''$ RADIUS

4"

2"

TYPE 2

120°

1"   K

8 7 6 5
4
3
2
1

8
7
6
5
4
3
2
1

$\frac{1}{4}''$

1 2 3 4 5 6 7 8

1"

DIAMETER $3\frac{5}{8}''$

Fig. 2

11

PLYWOOD ROLLER (type 2)

Cut the 16 plywood discs, in pairs, with the varying positions of the $\frac{1}{2}''$ deep slots as shown in Fig. 2. The slots must not be more than $\frac{1}{4}''$ wide. Each disc, it will be seen, has three slots, and each pair of discs has its slots in a different position in relation to the central square hole. The slots in the first pair of discs are at positions No. 1, the slots in the second pair of discs at positions No. 2, as shown. Take the first disc of pair numbered one, and place it on to a piece of 1″ square scrap wood. Take the second one of the pair, turn it over and thread on to the 1″ square wood so that the slots lie centrally between the slots of the first piece. Repeat with the remaining seven pairs and a flow pattern will result. This may sound like a Chinese puzzle but is quite simple once assembly has begun. Check that the slots lie in the correct position, apply glue between each disc, cramp up and remove the 1″ square centrepiece that has been used to line up the discs. Leave until the glue hardens then apply Araldite to each tooth and drive into position.

SPINDLE

Fix the four bearing pieces to the spindle (*H*) with Araldite to the position shown in Fig. 1 and shape as in section three. This is best cut on a lathe but can be shaped with a chisel and file. The spindle end (section 1) can be achieved by the same method.

SPINDLE ARM AND HANDLE

Cut the spindle arm (*I*) to shape, drill a $\frac{5}{8}''$ diameter hole for the handle and make a 1″ square hole to house section four of the spindle. Glue the spindle and $\frac{5}{8}''$ dowel into position.

PRESSURE ARM AND RAM ASSEMBLY

Cut the pressure arm (*G*) to shape and drill two $\frac{1}{4}''$ holes as indicated. Assemble the ram arm from pieces *J* and *K*, shape up part *L* and dowel and glue to ram arm. Drill a $\frac{1}{4}''$ hole through pieces *J* as shown.

CONTAINER BODY

Glue and screw the container back (*E*) to the cramping piece (*F*), the sides (*B*) to container front (*A*) and the back

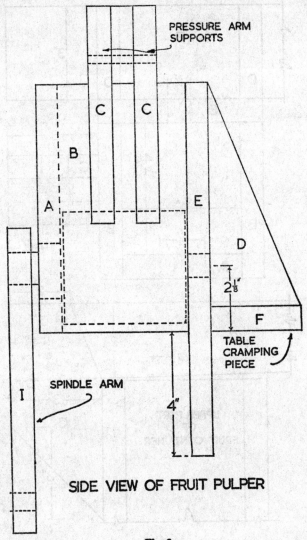

SIDE VIEW OF FRUIT PULPER

Fig. 3

13

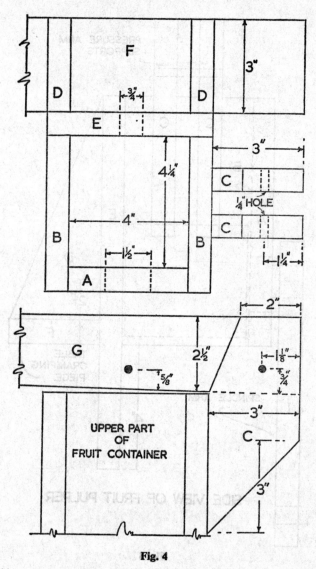

Fig. 4

14

(E) to the sides (B). Mark out carefully and bore the spindle holes as shown in Fig. 2. Cut the pressure arm supports (C) to shape and glue and screw to piece B, drill the $\frac{1}{4}''$ holes so that the pressure arm (G) lies centrally across the top of the fruit container. The back supports are made by cutting the $7'' \times 3''$ pieces (D) diagonally and are fixed to pieces E and F with glue and screws.

Rub down and apply at least three coats of polyurethane varnish.

CUTTING LIST

Note: All sizes given are finished sizes and must be strictly adhered to, otherwise the machine will not function smoothly and efficiently.

1 off $8'' \times 4'' \times \frac{3}{4}''$ / 152mm $\times$ 102mm $\times$ 19mm. (Container front A.)

2 off $8'' \times 5'' \times \frac{3}{4}''$ / 152mm $\times$ 127mm $\times$ 19mm. (Container sides B.)

2 off $7'' \times 3'' \times \frac{3}{4}''$ / 178mm $\times$ 76mm $\times$ 19mm. (Pressure arm suports C.)

1 off $7'' \times 3'' \times \frac{3}{4}''$ / 178mm $\times$ 76mm $\times$ 19mm. (Back supports, cut diagonally D.)

1 off $12'' \times 5\frac{1}{2}'' \times \frac{3}{4}''$ / 305mm $\times$ 140mm $\times$ 19mm. (Container back E.)

1 off $11\frac{1}{2}'' \times 3 \times \frac{3}{4}''$ / 292mm $\times$ 76mm $\times$ 19mm. (Cramping piece F.)

1 off. $17\frac{1}{2}'' \times 2\frac{1}{2}'' \times \frac{3}{4}''$ / 444mm $\times$ 63mm $\times$ 19mm. (Pressure arm, cut to shape G.)

1 off $6\frac{3}{4}'' \times 1'' \times 1''$ / 171mm $\times$ 25mm $\times$ 25mm. (Spindle H.)

1 off $10\frac{1}{2}'' \times 2'' \times \frac{3}{4}''$ / 267mm $\times$ 51mm $\times$ 19mm. (Spindle arm I.)

2 off $5'' \times 1\frac{1}{2}'' \times \frac{1}{2}''$ / 127mm $\times$ 38mm $\times$ 13mm. (Ram arms, cut to shape J.)

1 off $3\frac{1}{4}'' \times 1\frac{1}{2}'' \times \frac{7}{8}''$ / 82mm $\times$ 38mm $\times$ 22mm. (Ram arm spacer, cut to shape K.)

1 off $4'' \times 4'' \times 2''$ / 102mm $\times$ 102mm $\times$ 51mm. (Ram, cut to shape L.)

1 off $6'' \times \frac{5}{8}''$ dowel / 152mm $\times$ 16mm. (Spindle arm handle.)

4 off $1'' \times \frac{3}{4}'' \times \frac{3}{8}''$ / 25mm $\times$ 19mm $\times$ 9mm. (Spindle bearing.)

15

Roller (type 1)

4 off $4\frac{1}{8}'' \times 3'' \times 2''$ / 105mm × 76mm × 51mm.

1 off $4\frac{1}{8}'' \times 1'' \times 1''$ / 105mm × 25mm × 25mm.(Centre core for turning, later discarded.)

48 off $\frac{5}{8}'' \times \frac{3}{16}'' \times \frac{3}{16}''$ / 16mm × 5mm × 5mm. (Mild steel bar for teeth.)

or Roller (type 2)

$\frac{1}{4}''$ / 6mm plywood to cut 16 circles $3\frac{5}{8}''$ / 92mm diameter.

$\frac{1}{8}''$ / 3mm plywood to cut 2 circle $3\frac{5}{8}''$ / 92mm diameter.

48 off $\frac{3}{4}'' \times \frac{1}{4}'' \times \frac{1}{4}''$ / 19mm × 6mm × 6mm. (Mild steel bar for teeth.)

$1\frac{1}{2}''$ and $2''$ / 38mm and 51mm 8 gauge countersunk wood-screws, Araldite adhesive, two $2\frac{1}{2}'' \times \frac{1}{4}''$ bolts and wing nuts, $\frac{1}{4}''$ / 6mm dowelling. Two small thumb cramps.

Hand Fruit Crusher

One of the easiest methods of crushing hard fruit such as apples or pears is to use this simple type of crusher. It consists of a 9″ length of oak and a 2′ 6″ length of ash broom handle. The piece of oak can normally be obtained as an off-cut from a fencing contractor, ideally, free from shakes and knots. After cleaning up the four sides, mark and saw the ends square. Mark the centre on one of the ends and bore a 1″ diameter hole at least 3″ deep. Cut a 2′ 6″ length off the broom handle and cut three small grooves 3″ long on the end to be inserted in the oak block. These grooves will allow air and surplus glue to escape when the handle is driven home. Apply glue to the inside of the hole and to the grooved part of the handle and hammer the handle into the block. To prevent the handle coming loose drill a $\frac{1}{4}''$ diameter hole, $1\frac{1}{2}''$ down from the handle end of the block, as shown in Fig. 5 and glue up a 4″ length of $\frac{1}{4}''$ dowel and drive in.

16

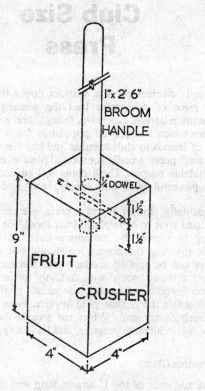

Fig. 5

Clean off surplus glue and dowel ends, glasspaper off sharp corners. This crusher should only be used in heavy duty containers such as wooden tubs and heavy-gauge flat-bottomed polythene buckets.

TOOLS REQUIRED

Handsaw, brace and bit, plane, rule, trysquare, hammer, drill and bits.

Club Size
Press

A really efficient press is without doubt the most useful single piece of equipment that the winemaker can own. Presses are relatively expensive, though, and a solution to the problem which has proved popular is for a wine circle or group of friends to club together and buy the materials for a "club size" press, a really substantial piece of equipment with a formidable output. These plans will enable you to make such a powerful press quite simply, easily and inexpensively.

Incidentally, do not expect a press, even one like this, to crush hard fruit to a pulp. All fruit should be pulped before pressing to obtain the maximum juice extraction and to prevent straining the press. One should not see how much pressure can be applied suddenly, for this can only lead to disaster; a small press will certainly be strained. With small commercial and home-made presses gradual pressure is used to obtain the highest yield of juice. Press until the juice runs freely, then stop. When the stream dies away to a dribble, again increase pressure, and leave to run again.

Construction (Base)

Mitre the ends of the 1″ square strip and fix them to the main base piece, using the $1\frac{1}{2}″ \times 8$ gauge screws and waterproof glue. Note the two long pieces on the underside are kept approximately $\frac{3}{8}″$ in from the edge to allow piece A to finish flush with edge of the base.

Cut and bend the metal pieces to the shapes as detailed in Fig. 6. At this stage the holes should be drilled, but we found it easier, not being precision engineers, to drill through two pieces of metal, when in place, to get the necessary accuracy.

Commence by marking and drilling holes in the centre of the base supports and in the lower ends of the bridge piece.

Fix together with the $\frac{1}{4}''$ bolts. Cut recesses in the 1" square strips on the underside of the base, to accommodate the nuts and protruding ends of the bolt. With the wooden base resting on its supports, drill and screw the corner ties into position. Offer the corner tie and bridge connecting piece in position, mark, drill and bolt to the bridge. Check the corner ties are at the correct angle and drill and bolt in place.

Form a hole large enough to take the bench screw in the centre of the bridge and bridge strengthener. This can be done by drilling a series of small holes in a circle and with their sides touching. Finish off with a round file. The bench screw nut is fixed to the underside of the bridge strengthener with the bolts passing through the bridge, thereby securing the three pieces together. A $1\frac{1}{4}''$ diameter hole is cut in the cover, to accommodate the bench screw thread, and fixed in position with the self tapping screws.

Construction of the pressure plate

To form the pressure plate, glue two of the oak discs together with their grain running at right-angles to each other. With the discs placed in the press and a suitable packing piece on top, the bench screw can be used to give the necessary pressure whilst the glue is hardening, then the cuphooks and pressure pieces can be fixed in position. The cuphooks screwed to the top of the pressure plate provides for easy removal of the plate after pressing.

Drum

Mark and drill 17 holes $1\frac{7}{8}''$ centres in both of the mild steel bands, starting with the first hole 1" from the end. It is easier to fix the hardwood strips with the bands flat. Start by laying out 15 hardwood strips on a flat surface approximately $\frac{3}{8}''$ apart. Lay the mild steel bands so that the second hole registers with the centre of the first slat and 1" from the ends; fix with the $\frac{1}{2}''$ screws. Fix the remaining 14 slats using the same method and positions. Form a circle with the bands on the outside of the slats, temporarily bolt the first and last holes together, mark, drill and rivet together. Remove the bolts and screw the last oak strip into position.

Thoroughly coat all surfaces with polyurethane varnish as detailed in Chapter 1.

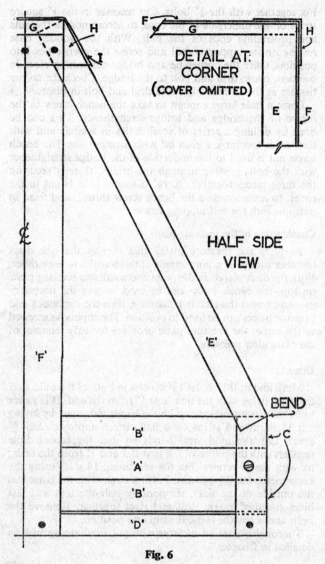

DETAIL AT: CORNER
(COVER OMITTED)

HALF SIDE VIEW

BEND

Fig. 6

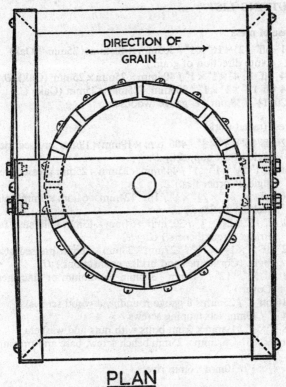

DIRECTION OF GRAIN

PLAN

COVER PIECE & FIXING BOLTS
OMITTED FOR CLARITY

Fig. 7

Tools required

Hand or panel saw, tenon saw, coping or padsaw, plane, rasp or spokeshave, chisels, drill and bits, bradawl, hammer, rule, trysquare, screwdriver, hacksaw, adjustable spanner, tinshears, file, mitre block and centre punch.

CUTTING LIST

Base of press

1 off $12'' \times 16'' \times 1''$ / 305mm $\times$ 406mm $\times$ 25mm (Oak) *A*. (Note direction of grain.)

4 off $1'\ 4'' \times 1'' \times 1''$ / 406mm $\times$ 25mm $\times$ 25mm (Oak) *B*.

4 off $12'' \times 1'' \times 1''$ / 305mm $\times$ 25mm $\times$ 25mm (Oak) *C*.

20 $1\frac{1}{2}''$ / 38mm $\times$ 8 gauge woodscrews.

Press (metal work)

2 off $16'' \times \frac{3}{4}'' \times \frac{3}{4}''$ / 406 mm $\times$ 19mm $\times$ 19mm pressed steel angle. (Base support.) *D*.

4 off $1'\ 5\frac{1}{2}'' \times 1'' \times 1''$ / 445mm $\times$ 25mm $\times$ 25mm pressed steel angle. (Corner ties.) *E*.

1 off $3'\ 8\frac{1}{4}'' \times 2\frac{1}{2}'' \times \frac{1}{8}''$ / 1m 124mm $\times$ 64mm $\times$ 3mm mild steel bar (Bridge.) *F*.

1 off $12'' \times 2\frac{1}{2}'' \times \frac{1}{2}''$ / 305mm $\times$ 64mm $\times$ 13mm mild steel bar (Bridge strengtheners.) *G*.

2 off $5'' \times 1\frac{1}{2}'' \times 1\frac{1}{2}''$ / 127mm $\times$ 38mm $\times$ 38mm pressed steel angle. (Corner ties and bridge connections.) *H*.

1 off $5\frac{5}{8}'' \times 12''$ / 143mm $\times$ 305mm aluminium or zinc sheet (Cover.) *I*

16 off $1''$ / 25mm $\times$ 8 gauge roundhead wood screws.

4 $\frac{1}{2}''$ / 13mm self tapping screws.

8 $\frac{3}{4}'' \times \frac{1}{4}''$ / 19mm $\times$ 6mm bolts with nuts and washers.

1 $16'' \times 1''$ / 406mm $\times$ 25mm bench screw, base and pressure pieces.

4 $\frac{3}{8}'' \times \frac{1}{4}''$ / 10mm $\times$ 6mm rivets.

Drum (woodwork)

16 off $10'' \times 1\frac{1}{2}'' \times \frac{3}{4}''$ / 254mm $\times$ 38mm $\times$ 19mm oak, planed to shape.

2 off $7\frac{3}{4}''$ / 197mm diameter $\times 1''$ / 25mm oak. (Drum pressure and draining plates.)

Metalwork

2 off $32'' \times \frac{1}{4}'' \times \frac{1}{16}''$ / 813mm $\times$ 6mm $\times$ 2mm galvanised mild steel strip.

32, $\frac{1}{2}''$ / 13mm $\times$ 6 gauge roundhead sheridised screws.

2 plastic coated cuphooks.

Stand for Club Size Press

The press may be stood on a table when in use, but you will find this stand to be the correct working height for the operator, also just right for the juice to discharge into a funnel in the neck of a gallon jar.

Cutting list

4 off 1' 6″ × 2″ × 2″ / 457mm × 51mm × 51mm softwood. (Legs.)

4 off 1' 4½″ × 2″ × 1″ / 419mm × 51mm × 51mm softwood. (Top and bottom rails, sides.)

4 off 1' 1″ × 2″ × 1″ / 330mm × 51mm × 25mm softwood. (Top and bottom rails, ends.)

2 off 1' 6″ × 1½″ × ¾″ / 457mm × 38mm × 19mm softwood. (Top mouldings.)

2 off 1' 2½″ × 1½″ × ¾″ / 369mm × 38mm × 19mm softwood. (Top mouldings.)

32 2″ / 51mm × 8 gauge countersunk woodscrews.
1½″ / 38mm oval nails.

Construction

Mitre the ends of the top and bottom rails and screw them to the ends of the legs to form a table as shown in Fig. 8. The moulding, which retains the press base, is then mitred and fitted so that it projects ½″ above the rails.

A packing piece about ⅜″ thick may be fitted to one end of the stand to tilt the press and help clear the juice.

Tools required

Handsaw, tenon saw, plane, drill and bits, hammer, rule, trysquare, bradawl, screwdriver, mitre block, nail punch.

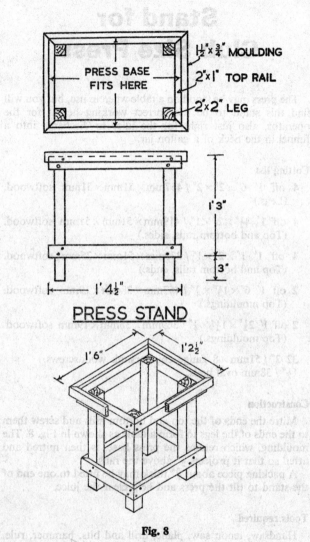

PRESS STAND

½" x ¾" MOULDING

2" x 1" TOP RAIL

PRESS BASE FITS HERE

2" x 2" LEG

1'3"

3"

1'4½"

1'6"

1'2½"

Fig. 8

Small Press

A small press is very useful to every winemaker. This
model, although costing little to make, is extremely efficient.
A vice screw 16″ long is used to give the required pressure,
but a modern car jack, hydraulic or screw type, could be
used with slight modification to the pressure beam (*A*). We
recommend a Record or Woden vice screw, 16″ long, obtainable from any good ironmonger.

Cut the two end pressure pieces to the shape shown and
glue and dowel (or screw) the 9″ long hardwood battens to
the faces of these pieces. Take the two side pieces and glue
and dowel (or screw) these between the end pieces (*B*). Affix
the smaller hardwood strips to the bottom edges of the sides
and ends with glue and dowels (or screws). While the glue is
hardening cut out the bottom perforated board and plane the
edges until it is a loose fit (about $\frac{1}{8}$″ clearance all round is
about right) in the bottom of the press. Mark out and drill
25 $\frac{1}{2}$″ diameter holes in this plate. Glue the top pressure plates
together and leave to set.

If using a vice screw, drill a $1\frac{1}{8}$″ diameter hole through a
12″ length of 3″ × 2″ hardwood, place the hardwood through
the oblong cut-outs in the ends, remove the nut from the
screw thread, place in the bored hole, replace the nut and the
press is ready for use.

A hydraulic jack only requires packing pieces to be placed
on the pressure plate to bring the jack up to a 12″ long × 3″ × 2″
oak pressure beam. A crank arm would be needed to work
the jack.

The pressure beam for use with a modern screw type car jack, (Fig. 9) consists of two sections and is constructed out of two 12″ lengths of 3″ × 1″ hardwood (D), and a 12″ × 3″ × ⅜″ thick plywood (E). The plywood is glued from its centre to one end on one side and from the centre to the other end on the reverse. Cramp up and allow the glue to harden. Drill a hole through the hardwood and plywood packing piece, slightly larger than the diameter of the jack. You should then have two pieces of wood each with a plywood piece glued to it. Chamfer off the inside face of one of the hardwood pieces and cut back the plywood packing as shown. The pulp to be pressed is placed in the press, the top pressure plates placed in position, then one part of the beam is inserted into the oblong holes, the jack placed in position and the other beam piece is inserted from the top. The chamfered surfaces may require trimming to make assembly easier.

A tray is needed under the press to collect the juice and it is made from the remaining lengths of hardwood which are mitred, glued and pinned to the edges of the thin plywood. A hole is drilled at the point of the base large enough to take a short length of polythene tube. All surfaces are rubbed down with coarse and fine glasspaper, dusted off and given three coats of polyurethane. Particular care must be taken to ensure that the varnish covers the inside of the holes in the bottom pressure plate to prevent the entry of bacteria.

Cutting list

The following in exterior quality plywood:
- 2 off 18″ × 11″ × ¾″ / 457mm × 279mm × 19mm. (Ends.)
- 2 off 9″ × 8″ × ¾″ / 229mm × 203mm × 19mm. (Sides.)
- 2 off 8″ × 8″ × ¾″ / 203mm × 203mm × 19mm. (Top and bottom pressure plates.)
- 1 off 6″ × 6″ × ¾″ / 152mm × 152mm × 19mm. (Top of pressure plate.)
- 2 off 12″ × 3″ × 1″ / 305mm × 76mm × 25mm. (hardwood.)
- 1 off 12″ × 3″ × 2″ / 305mm × 76mm × 51mm (hardwood.) (Pressure beam. For vice screw or hydraulic jack.)
- 4 off 9″ × 1″ × 1″ / 229mm × 25mm × 25mm hardwood. (Side supports.)

4 off 8" × 1" × 1" / 203mm × 25mm × 25mm hardwood. (Bottom supports.)

¼" hardwood dowel or 1½" × 8" / 38mm countersunk wood screws and glue.

Base tray

1 off 12" × 14" × ¼" / 305mm × 356mm × 6mm. (Exterior quality plywood.)

3 off 12" × 2" × ½" / 305mm × 25mm × 13mm (hardwood.

2 off 6" × 2" × ½" / 152mm × 25mm × 13mm hardwood.

Tools required

Hand or panel saw, coping or pad saw, plane, chisels, drill and bits, bradawl, hammer, rule, trysquare and screwdriver.

SMALL PRESS PRESSURE BAR

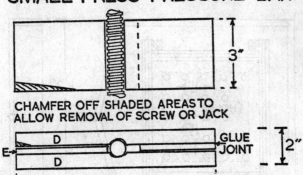

CHAMFER OFF SHADED AREAS TO ALLOW REMOVAL OF SCREW OR JACK

Fig. 9

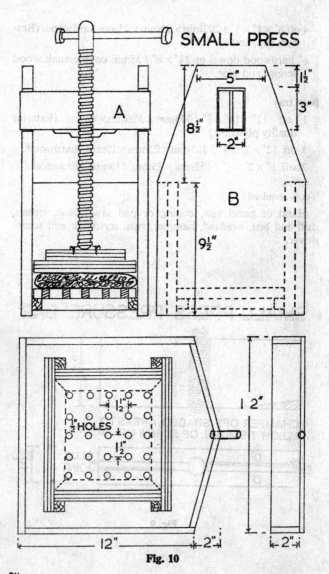

SMALL PRESS

A

B

1½"
5"
3"
2"
8½"
9½"

12"
1½"
½" HOLES
1½"
12"
2"
12"
2"
2"

Fig. 10

28

Simple Weighing Balance

This easily made balance should prove useful for measuring out small quantities of sugar, etc., and, no doubt, there are household uses to which it could be put also.

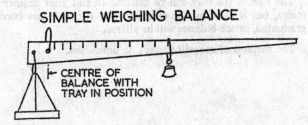

SIMPLE WEIGHING BALANCE

CENTRE OF
BALANCE WITH
TRAY IN POSITION

Fig. 11

What you need

Nothing more is needed than the lid from a tin or something similar, to be used as a tray, a weight of about $1\frac{1}{2}$ oz., a piece of wood about $18''$ long $\times \frac{1}{4}'' \times 1\frac{1}{2}''$, and some cord or wire. None of these measurements is critical, and they are given just as a guide.

The wood should be cut so that it tapers from $1\frac{1}{2}''$ at one end to about $\frac{1}{4}''$ at the other. Two holes are drilled as indicated, the first being $\frac{1}{4}''$ from the end of the wood, and the other at approximately the centre of the balance. The tray is suspended from the first of these, and the second is the hole through which wire or cord is passed to act as a fulcrum.

Fixing the weight

The weight, which will probably need to be about $1\frac{1}{2}$ oz., must be threaded or fastened with wire so that it can be hung from the long arm of the balance. Be sure to fasten it in such a way that it slides easily along the arm.

For the marking of the scale it is necessary to use some articles the weight of which is known. Place them in the tray and move the weight along until a position is reached where the balance hangs with the arm in a horizontal position clearly on the side of the arm. Repeat this with other known weights, such as an unopened packet of tea, until the limit of the arm is reached. It will be realised that with one weight of 1 oz., one of 2 oz., and one of 3 oz., all even ounce markings up to 6 can be obtained. No doubt you can soon obtain the intermediate markings, and those of $\frac{1}{2}$ lb. and above.

The size of the tray can be selected to suit your requirements, but it must not be changed after the scale has been graduated, or the balance will be altered.

The method of use will present no difficulties.

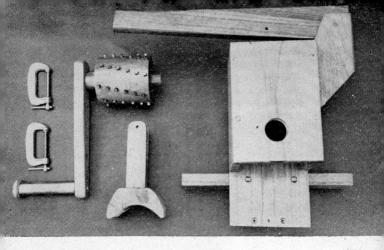

This sturdy pulper will
quickly and easily reduce
hard fruit, such as apples,
to a slurry

Traditional style basket press; ideal for club use.

Simply constructed fruit press; can be built in an evening and gives many years service

Racking and straining stand fitted to the inside of a cupboard door

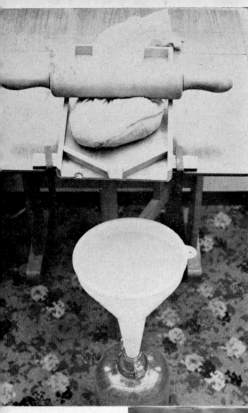

A pulp squeezer is ideal for extracting juice from pulp after soaking

Useful items of equipment

Left to Right
Cork flogger
Hand fruit-crusher
Floating siphon
Carboy trolley
Large stirrer
Plonker
Bottle corking holder

Large and Small Stirrers

As Fig. 12 shows, a simply made stirrer for rousing beer or stirring pulp in winemaking can be made from a $3' \times 3'' \times 1''$ piece of oak. The waste pieces cut off after forming the handle are added to the paddle section to give extra width.

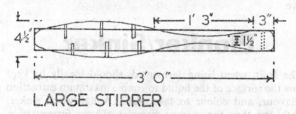

LARGE STIRRER

Fig. 12

Mark out the handle and cut with a coping, pad or bow saw. Glue the waste pieces to the opposite end to form the paddle shape. Cramp up and drill three holes $\frac{3}{8}''$ diameter and $2''$ deep through each of the waste pieces into the body part. Drive into these holes a $2''$ length of dowel coated with waterproof glue. When the glue has hardened, shape edges with a spokeshave or rasp and finish off with glasspaper. After drilling a $\frac{1}{4}''$ diameter hole for a hanging cord through the handle, dust off and apply polyurethane clear varnish.

A $12''$ length of leather thong, bootlace or nylon cord passed through the hole in the handle and tied to form a hanging loop completes this item.

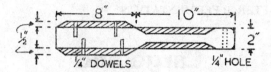

SMALL STIRRER

Fig. 13

The small stirrer is constructed in the same way from a piece of hardwood to dimensions shown in Fig. 13.

Tools required

Saw, coping saw, brace, drill bits, hammer, rasp or spokeshave.

Plonker/Sinker

The fruit, when being fermented, should ideally be kept below the surface of the liquid to enable maximum extraction of flavour, and colour to take place. A hardwood sinker, slightly less than the average diameter of your fermentation vessel, will help to fulfil these conditions. To find the most suitable size for your sinker, measure the diameter at the top and bottom of your fermentation vessel, add these dimensions together and divide by two; this will give you the right diameter to allow the sinker to keep the fruit below the surface providing the bucket is at least half full of must.

Mark out the required size circle on a 1″ thick piece of hardwood, preferably oak, and cut out with a coping saw. Two or more pieces of timber may be joined together, edge to edge, to give the necessary width. See Fig. 14. The 1″ × 2″ pieces of hardwood are waterproof glued and dowelled across the grain to give added strength. Bore the ½″ and ¾″ diameter holes, clean up with coarse and fine glasspaper and apply polyurethane varnish, making sure the inside surfaces of the holes are well coated. A suitable sized weight wrapped in a polythene bag will keep the sinker below the surface.

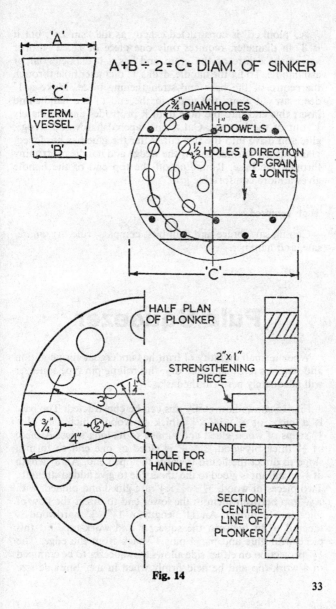

A+B ÷ 2 = C = DIAM. OF SINKER

'A'

'C'

FERM.
VESSEL

'B'

¾" DIAM. HOLES

¼" DOWELS

½" HOLES   DIRECTION
OF GRAIN
& JOINTS

'C'

HALF PLAN
OF PLONKER

2"x1"
STRENGTHENING
PIECE

1¼"

3

¾"   ½"

4"

HANDLE

HOLE FOR
HANDLE

SECTION
CENTRE
LINE OF
PLONKER

Fig. 14

A "plonker" is constructed exactly as the "sinker", but it is 8″ in diameter, requires only one piece of 1″ × 2″ timber across the centre of the grain and has a 1″ diameter oak or ash handle. To fix the handle, drill a 1″ diameter hole through the centre of the base and strengthening piece. Make a 1″ deep saw cut along the grain in the end of the handle and insert this end into the hole until it protrudes approximately ⅛″ out of the bottom. Cut a fine tapered hardwood wedge, glue and drive into the saw cut. After the glue has hardened, plane off the surplus end of the wedge and handle protruding through the base. Rounding off the top end of the handle gives a more comfortable grip.

Tools required

Coping saw, brace and drill bits, compass, rule, trysquare, saw, and hammer.

Pulp Squeezer

When a small quantity of fruit has undergone fermentation and requires to be squeezed dry, this rolling pin type squeezer will adequately perform the task.

Fig. 15 shows how easily this can be constructed. The base is a piece of 8″ × 14″ × ¼″ thick plywood which has ¾″ × ½″ strips of wood glued and pinned to its long sides. A piece of ¼″ thick plywood, 3″ × 8″ is glued to one end to form a slope to direct the liquid towards the open end. An 8″ length of ½″ quadrant is glued to the underside to give added strength. Two pieces of wood, 3¾″ × ¾″ × ½″ are glued and pinned, with a ¾″ gap between them in the lower end to direct the flow of juice into a funnel. An 11″ length of 1½″ × ½″ hardwood is tapered to fit between the squeezer and work-top. Fit this piece with glue and panel pins 1″ back from the edge. The 1½″ projection on either side allows the squeezer to be cramped to a work-top and be held firmly when in use. Suitable size

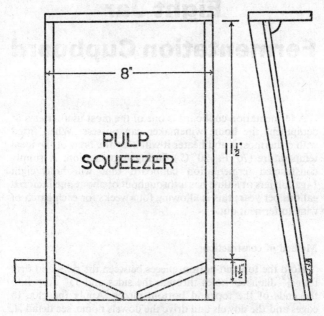

Fig. 15

pressed steel thumb screw cramps are readily available from most D.I.Y. shops, ironmongers, department stores, etc.

Rub down all sharp edges with glasspaper, punch in all nail heads, dust off and apply at least three coats of polyurethane.

To use, cramp the squeezer to a work-top and place a jar and funnel under the outlet end. The pulp, in a muslin bag, is placed on the base and allowed to drain for a few moments. It is then squeezed dry with a rolling pin moved up and down using the side pieces as a guide. Turning the bag at intervals will assist better extraction of juice.

Tools required

Panel or tenon saw, plane, hammer, rule, trysquare, nail punch.

35

Eight Jar
Fermentation Cupboard

A fermentation cupboard is one of the most useful items of equipment the home winemaker can possess. When fitted with a thermostat and heater it will keep the brew at the ideal temperature (70° F., 20° C.) during fermentation. A simply constructed fermentation cupboard that will hold eight 1-gallon jars at a time has a throughput of about one hundred gallons per year; this is allowing four weeks for each batch of wine to ferment out.

Method of construction

Hold the top and bottom pieces between the sides and drill four $\frac{1}{4}''$ diameter holes through the sides and $1\frac{1}{4}''$ deep into the ends of the top and bottom pieces. Apply the glue to edges and the dowels and drive the dowels home, see detail A, Fig. 17. Check for squareness, adjust as necessary and leave until the glue hardens. Mark out position of the shelves, drill $\frac{1}{4}''$ diameter holes through the sides and 1″ deep into the ends of the shelves. Glue and dowel as shown in detail B. Glue and pin the shelf supports to the front and back edges, in the centre of the shelves. Cut 2, 5″ square pieces diagonally and drill, glue and dowel, as shown in detail C, in the corners flush with the back edges. These pieces are drilled and used as fixing blocks and also serve to give strength to the unit. Glue and pin the hardboard to the back edges and trim off flush. Drill screw fixing holes through the hardboard and corner blocks. Cut in the hinges 3″ from the top and bottom and screw hinges to door panels and side members.

Fix the self-adhesive foam draught excluder to the front edges of the cabinet so that it is compressed when the doors are closed.

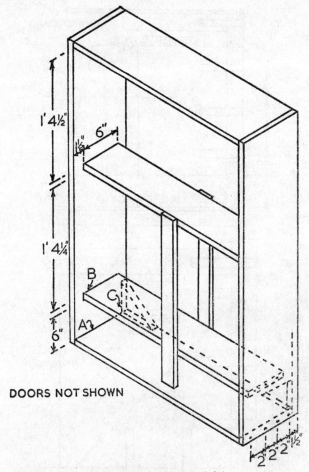

1' 4½"

6"

⅛"

1' 4¼"

B

C

A

6"

2" 2" 2½"

DOORS NOT SHOWN

8 JAR FERMENTATION
CUPBOARD

Fig. 16

37

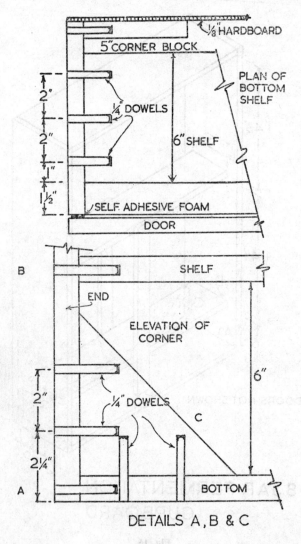

1/8" HARDBOARD
5" CORNER BLOCK
PLAN OF BOTTOM SHELF
DOWELS
1/4 DOWELS
6" SHELF
2"
2"
1"
1/2"
SELF ADHESIVE FOAM
DOOR

B
SHELF
END
ELEVATION OF CORNER
1/4" DOWELS
2"
C
6"
2 1/4"
A
BOTTOM

DETAILS A, B & C

Fig. 17

Wire up the batten lamp holders in parallel and thermostat as shown in the electric detail and screw into position as shown in Fig. 18.

Finishing

Rub all raw edges and dowels with coarse and fine glasspaper, dust off and apply paint, or polish with polyurethane to suit existing colour schemes. Fit cupboard catches and door handles.

The cupboard may be plugged and screwed to a wall or stood on a suitable surface near a power point, plug in, set the thermostat to 70° F. (20° C.) and the cabinet is then ready for use.

Suitable materials

"Contiboard"; $\frac{3}{4}''$ / 19mm blockboard; $\frac{3}{4}''$ / 19mm plywood.

Cutting list

2 off 2' $4\frac{1}{2}'' \times 9'' \times \frac{3}{4}''$ / 724mm × 229mm × 19mm. (Top and bottom.)

2 off 3' $6'' \times 9'' \times \frac{3}{4}''$ / 1m 67mm × 229mm × 19mm. (Sides.)

2 off 2' $4\frac{1}{2}'' \times 6'' \times \frac{3}{4}''$ / 724mm × 152mm × 19mm. (Shelves.)

2 off 3' 6'' × 1' 3'' × $\frac{3}{4}''$ / 1m 67mm × 381mm × 19mm. (Doors.)

44 2'' / 51mm × $\frac{1}{4}''$ / 6mm hardwood dowels.

2 off 2' $\frac{1}{2}'' \times 2'' \times \frac{1}{2}''$ / 623mm × 51mm × 13mm softwood. (Shelf supports.)

4 off corner blocks, cut diagonally from 2, 5'' / 127mm squares of $\frac{3}{4}''$ / 19mm material.

2 pairs, 2'' / 51mm hinges and screws.

2 cupboard catches.

2 knobs or handles to choice.

1 off $\frac{1}{8}''$ / 3mm hardboard 2' 6'' × 3' 6'' / 762mm × 1m 67mm. (Back.)

$\frac{3}{4}''$ / 19mm hardboard fixing pins.

Wood glue, 12' / 3m 658mm of self adhesive foam strip (Draught excluder.)

Thermostat—airtype, 2 batten type lamp holders and screws. (Thermostat available from Vina, page 118.)

2 lamps (See electrical section on p. 40.)

Tools required

Trysquare, brace and drill bits, rule, panel or handsaw, hammer, plugging chisel or rawplugging tool, screwdriver, nail punch, plane.

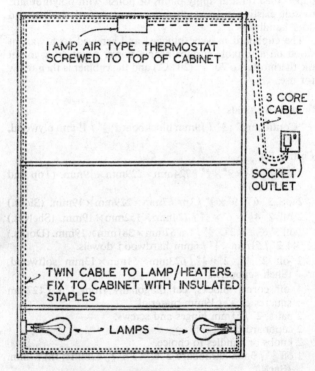

WIRING DIAGRAM FOR

FERMENTATION CUPBOARD

Fig. 18

Four Jar
Fermentation Cupboard

For some winemakers a four jar fermentation cupboard will be adequate as this size allows a throughput of approximately 50 gallons a year. It is basically constructed on the same principle as the 8 jar size but with the following alterations. The top, bottom and shelves are 1' 3" long. Only one door is fitted and this is 3' 6" high by 1' 4½" wide. No centre shelf supports are needed and only one door handle, one cupboard catch, one batten lamp holder and one pair of hinges are required. The hardboard back is 3' 6" × 1' 4½" wide.

Method of construction

Follow the same method as for the 8 jar cupboard but incorporating the above variations. The door may be hung on the left or right-hand side.

Six Jar
Fermentation Cupboard

Winemakers with limited space in the home for fermenting wine in gallon jars will find this cabinet, fixed externally, to be the answer. This cabinet is designed to withstand the elements and may even be fixed on a north facing wall. Legs could be added to make it free-standing, but it would need a fixing into a wall to give stability. If positioned near a window it will be easier, and cheaper, to run the electricity supply to it as a small hole can usually be drilled through the window frame to accommodate the cable.

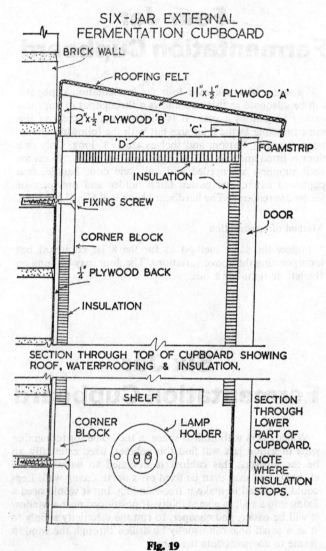

SIX-JAR EXTERNAL
FERMENTATION CUPBOARD

BRICK WALL

ROOFING FELT

11" x ½" PLYWOOD 'A'

2" x ½" PLYWOOD 'B'

'C'

'D'

FOAMSTRIP

INSULATION

FIXING SCREW

DOOR

CORNER BLOCK

¼ PLYWOOD BACK

INSULATION

SECTION THROUGH TOP OF CUPBOARD SHOWING
ROOF, WATERPROOFING & INSULATION.

SHELF

SECTION
THROUGH
LOWER
PART OF
CUPBOARD.

CORNER
BLOCK

LAMP
HOLDER

NOTE
WHERE
INSULATION
STOPS.

Fig. 19

42

Construction

This cabinet is basically constructed on the same principle as the 8 jar size, but incorporating the above variations. After the cabinet is built the door, back, sides and top are lined with the polystyrene sheets or ceiling tiles if more convenient. The roof is added as shown in Fig. 19, painted, then covered with the roofing felt.

Strict adherence to the painting recommendations in Chapter 1 will ensure long life for this cabinet.

Cutting lists

Exterior quality plywood

  2 off 3' 6″ × 9″ × ¾″ / 1m 67mm × 229mm × 19mm. (Sides.)
  2 off 1' 10½″ × 9″ × ¾″ / 572mm × 229mm × 19mm. (Top and bottom.)
  2 off 1' 10½″ × 6″ × ¾″ / 572mm × 152mm × 19mm. (Shelves.)
  1 off 2' × 3' 6″ × ¼″ / 610mm × 1m 67mm × 19mm. (Door.)
  1 off 2' × 3' 6″ × ¼″ / 610mm × 1m 67mm × 6mm. (Back.)
  4 off corner blocks cut diagonally from 2, 5″ / 127mm squares ¾″ / 19mm thick.

Expanded polystyrene

  2 off 3' × 9″ × ½″ / 1m 143mm × 229mm × 13mm. (Sides.) (Cut out for shelves.)
  1 off 1' 9½″ × 9″ × ½″ / 546mm × 229mm × 13mm. (Top.)
  2 off 1' 9½″ × 3' × ½″ / 546mm × 914mm × 13mm. (Door and back.)

Miscellaneous

  1 off 2' 1″ × 11″ × ½″ / 635mm × 279mm × 13mm. (Exterior quality plywood.) *A*.
  1 off 2' 1″ × 2″ × ½″ / 635mm × 51mm × 13mm. (Exterior quality plywood.) *B*.
  2 off 7½″ × 2″ × ½″ / 191mm × 51mm × 13mm. (Exterior quality plywood cut to shape.) *D*.
  1 off 2' 1″ × 1″ × ½″ / 635mm × 26mm × 26mm. *C*
Half a yard of roofing felt and clout nails.
44 2″ × ¼″ / 51mm × 6mm hardwood dowels.
1 pair 3″ / 76mm hinges and screws.

1 strong cupboard catch.

1 knob or handle to choice

$\frac{3}{4}''$ / 19mm panel pins.

11′ self adhesive foam strip draught excluder.

Thermostat (air type).

2 batten type lamp holders, screws and wire.

2 lamps. (See electrical section, p. 40.)

Polystyrene adhesive.

Tools required

Panel saw, tenon saw, trysquare, rule, chisel, screwdriver, hammer, sharp knife, drill and bits, nail punch.

Carboy Trolley

Many a back has been strained through moving a full 10 gallon mashing bin or carboy. This can be prevented by fitting four castors to a piece of plywood to make this task a sheer delight.

To build this trolley, cut and clean up the edges of a $\frac{3}{4}''$ thick piece of plywood or blockboard and screw a plate fixing castor 1″ in from each corner as shown in Fig. 20. After glasspapering the base the appearance can be improved by applying a coat of priming paint, an undercoat, and a finishing coat.

Do not forget to put the carboy or bin on the trolley before filling.

Tools required

Handsaw, rule, bradawl, screwdriver, plane and square.

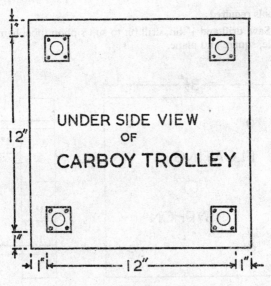

Fig. 20

Floating Siphon

When a third hand is not available to hold the end of the siphon tube at the correct distance from the yeast deposit, a floating siphon such as this is indispensable.

All you need is a 5″ square piece of 1″ thick hardwood and drill a $\frac{1}{4}$″ diameter hole in each corner, as shown in Fig. 21. Cut four 2″ lengths of $\frac{1}{4}$″ dowel and glue them into the holes. Drill a hole in the centre of the timber large enough to hold the end of the siphon tube securely.

As the level of the liquid in the bin falls the block descends with it, keeping the end of the siphon just below the surface. The four dowel legs rest on the yeast deposit, preventing it being sucked into the bottles. Finish with clear varnish as detailed in Chapter 1.

Tools required

Saw, drill and $\frac{1}{4}$″ bit, drill bit to suit siphon tube, hammer, rule, square and plane.

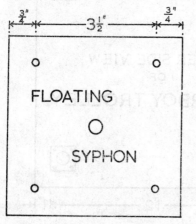
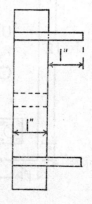

Fig. 21

Racking and Straining Stand

Although you can hang a straining bag from the legs of an upturned chair this is not really satisfactory. Similarly, a chair standing beside a table is not always the right height when racking and bottling. An adjustable stand such as we describe here, when fitted on to the inside face of a cupboard door, takes up very little room and can be adjusted to suit the job in hand.

We give below the method of making the entire structure from wood. The alternative would be to use the "Welpac" adjustable shelving system for which you would require two 3′ lengths of upright and two pairs of 8″ brackets. The uprights are fixed with the screws supplied in the same positions as the wooden vertical members, i.e. 9″ apart and 18″ from the floor. With the Welpac system you do not require the items marked with a star in the cutting list.

Cutting list

*2 off 3′ × 2″ × 1″ / 914mm × 51mm × 25mm. (Vertical members.)

* 4 off 9½″ × 2″ × 1″ / 241mm × 51mm × 25mm. (Shelf bearers A, cut to shape.)

* 4 off 3½″ × 2″ × 1″ / 89mm × 51mm × 25mm. (Shelf bearers B, cut to shape.)

* 8 off 8″ × 5½″ × ¼″ / 203mm × 140mm × 6mm plywood. (Shelf bearer plates, cut to shape.)

* 4 off 4″ × ¼″ / 102mm × 6mm dowel.

2 off 12″ × 9″ × ½″ / 305mm × 229mm × 13mm blockboard or plywood. (Racking shelves.)

2 off 12″ × 10″ × ¾″ / 305mm × 254mm × 13mm blockboard or plywood. (Straining bag and funnel holders.)

4 off 1½″ × ¼″ / 38mm × 6mm dowel. (Straining bag pegs.)

* 6 2½″ / 64mm × 10 gauge countersunk woodscrews.

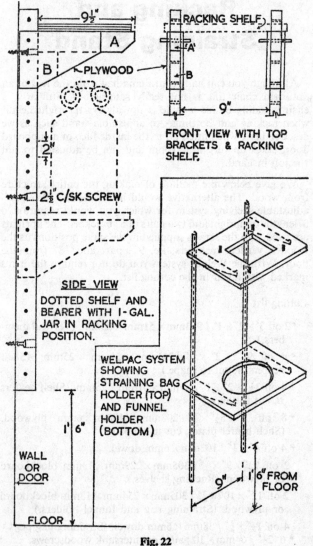

9½"

RACKING SHELF

A

B — PLYWOOD

A'

B

9"

FRONT VIEW WITH TOP BRACKETS & RACKING SHELF.

2"

2½" C/SK. SCREW

SIDE VIEW
DOTTED SHELF AND
BEARER WITH 1-GAL.
JAR IN RACKING
POSITION.

WELPAC SYSTEM
SHOWING
STRAINING BAG
HOLDER (TOP)
AND FUNNEL
HOLDER (BOTTOM)

1' 6"

WALL
OR
DOOR

FLOOR

9"

1' 6" FROM
FLOOR

Fig. 22

Construction

Cramp together the two vertical members, mark out and drill $\frac{5}{16}''$ diameter holes, $2''$ apart along the middle of the $2''$ face. Drill clearance holes through the timber, countersunk deeply to allow good fixing, and screw the verticals $9''$ apart on the inside face of the door with the $2\frac{1}{2}'' \times 10$ gauge screws. Keep the bottom of the pieces level and about $18''$ from the floor.

Assemble the shelf bearers as shown in Fig. 22, using glue and panel pins. Drill a $\frac{5}{16}''$ hole $1''$ down from the top in each of the plywood shelf bearer plates to correspond with the holes in the vertical members making sure shelf bearers B are pressed hard against the vertical members. If the shelf bearers are a tight fit rub down the faces of the verticals with coarse glasspaper until they slide freely.

Glasspaper all rough edges and place the brackets on the verticals using the $4'' \times \frac{1}{4}''$ dowels to retain them in position.

The racking shelves only need to be smoothed down with glasspaper, painted to choice and placed on the shelf bearers and they are then ready for use.

Holders for Straining Bag and Funnel

To make the funnel holder, find the centre of the $10'' \times 12''$ piece of blockboard or plywood by drawing lines connecting opposite corners. Mark a circle, using this centre point, of sufficient size to allow top rim of the funnel to rest on the board when the aperture has been cut. We used an $8''$ funnel which required an $8\frac{1}{8}''$ hole; check the outside diameter of your funnel just below the rim to find the correct size hole to cut. When the circle has been marked, cut carefully on the line. After smoothing with glasspaper apply three coats of polyurethane.

The straining bag holder is made by cutting a $6''$ square hole in the centre of the remaining piece of $10'' \times 12''$ block-board or plywood. Mark the positions of the holes to take the $\frac{1}{4}''$ dowels, drill and glue the dowels in place, Fig. 23. The

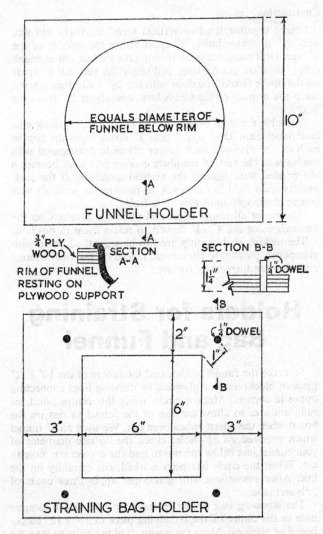

EQUALS DIAMETER OF
FUNNEL BELOW RIM

A

FUNNEL HOLDER

10"

3/4" PLY
WOOD

RIM OF FUNNEL
RESTING ON
PLYWOOD SUPPORT

SECTION
A-A

A

SECTION B-B

1 1/4"   1 1/4" DOWEL

B

2"   1/4" DOWEL

B

6"

1"

3"   6"   3"

STRAINING BAG HOLDER

Fig. 23

straining bags are retained by slipping the loops over these pegs, see Chapter 8 for modifying straining bags for use with this holder. Finish as for funnel holder.

To use

When straining, place a gallon jar on the floor, adjust the lower pair of brackets so that when the funnel, in its holder, is placed on them, the outlet of the funnel will discharge into the jar. Adjust the top brackets, which support the straining bag holder, so that the strained liquid drains into the funnel.

Tools required

Handsaw, tenon saw, drill, drill bits, countersunk bit, rule, hammer, square, screwdriver, bradawl, small cramps, compass, coping saw, plane.

Bottle Draining Stand

When you have a lot of bottles to wash, it is always tricky trying to stand them upside down on the average draining board; this stand will solve the problem.

Mark out the piece of plywood, preferably exterior, as sketched on Fig. 24. Drill $\frac{3}{8}''$ diameter holes at the centres shown. Using waterproof glue, drive a length of the $\frac{3}{8}''$ dowelling into each hole, flush with the underside of the plywood. Clean off surplus glue, leave to harden, and glass-paper the tops of the dowels to remove rough edges. Cut and mitre the corners of the $1\frac{1}{2}'' \times \frac{1}{2}''$ softwood strips to the top edge and the sides. Keeping the underside flush, glue and screw them into position. Fix the $1'' \times 1''$ batten to the underside, near the top edge, with glue and the $1\frac{1}{2}''$ screws. Finish off as described in Chapter 1.

BOTTLE DRAINING STAND

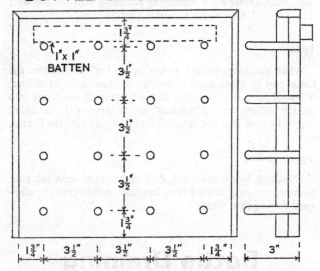

Fig. 24

Cutting list

1 off $14'' \times 14'' \times \frac{3}{4}''$ / 356mm × 356mm × 19mm exterior quality plywood.

3 off $15'' \times 1\frac{1}{2}'' \times \frac{1}{2}''$ / 381mm × 38mm × 13mm rounded top softwood.

1 off $12'' \times 1'' \times 1''$ / 305mm × 25mm × 25mm softwood.

1 off $4' \, 8'' \times \frac{3}{8}''$ / 1m 422mm × 10mm hardwood dowelling, cut into 16 pieces $3''$ / 76mm long.

12 $1''$ / 25mm × 8 gauge countersunk wood screws.

3 $1\frac{1}{2}''$ / 38mm × 8 gauge countersunk wood screws.

Waterproof glue.

To use

Place the stand on the draining board of the sink and put upturned, washed and sulphited bottles on the pegs. The bottle should lay at a slight angle to allow the solution to drain clear of the neck. The $1'' \times 1''$ piece of wood situated at the top end helps to allow the water to drain clear.

Tools required

Saw, plane, drill, countersunk and $\frac{3}{8}''$ drill bit, brace, hammer, screwdriver, square, bradawl, rule.

Bottle Corking Holder

Often an extra hand is required to steady the bottle when using a hand corker. If a base is built and cramped to a table this simplifies the operation.

Cut a $3\frac{1}{2}''$ diameter hole in pieces of wood $4\frac{1}{2}''$ square. Any $1''$ thick timber, plywood or blockboard is suitable. Glue and nail the pieces together, to form a block, and fix to the plywood base; Fig. 25 shows the position.

See Chapter 1 for finishing.

In use the holder may be held firmly to a table with two small size thumb cramps or placed on the floor and held down with your feet.

Cutting list

4 off $4\frac{1}{2}'' \times 4\frac{1}{2}'' \times 1''$ / 114mm $\times$ 114mm $\times$ 25mm timber.
1 off $8\frac{1}{2}'' \times 4\frac{1}{2}'' \times \frac{3}{8}''$ / 216mm $\times$ 114mm $\times$ 10mm plywood.
$1\frac{1}{2}''$ / 38mm nails, glue, 2 thumb cramps.

Tools required

Panel or tenon saw, coping, pad or bowsaw, hammer, punch, halfround rasp, drill and bit (to start circular hole), plane, square, rule and compass.

BOTTLE CORKING HOLDER

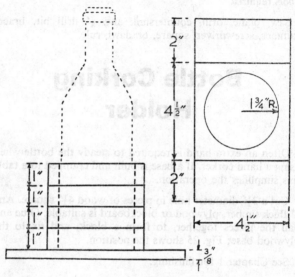

Fig. 25

Cork Flogger

A 12″ × 3″ × 1″ piece of hardwood with one end shaped to form a handle as shown in Fig. 26 is a very cheap and easy method of driving corks into a bottle. The corks will still have to be soaked to soften them and a piece of plastic coated or stainless steel wire placed in the bottle neck before the cork is inserted and when withdrawn, after corking, allows the air pressure to be released.

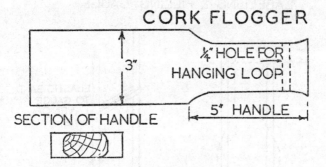

CORK FLOGGER

3"

¼" HOLE FOR HANGING LOOP

SECTION OF HANDLE

5" HANDLE

Fig. 26

Labelling and Filling Gauge

The only thing that looks worse than a batch of filled bottles with the wine at various levels is labels stuck on at different heights and angles. This simple gauge will enable all bottles to be filled to the same level in the neck and when laid on its back the gauge steadies the bottle and helps you to put the labels on squarely.

Cutting list

1 off $4'' \times 4'' \times \frac{1}{2}''$ / 102mm × 102mm × 13mm blockboard or plywood.

2 off $2\frac{1}{4}'' \times 1\frac{3}{4}'' \times \frac{1}{4}''$ / 59mm × 44mm × 6mm plywood (gauge for label).

2 off $12'' \times \frac{3}{8}''$ / 305mm × 10mm dowel.

2 $\frac{3}{4}''$ / 19mm screws, $\frac{3}{4}''$ / 19mm panel pins, wood glue, 1 elastic band.

Start by drilling the two $\frac{3}{8}''$ diameter holes $\frac{7}{8}''$ centre up from the bottom and $\frac{7}{8}''$ centre in from the sides. Glue the ends of the dowel and drive them into the holes. Attach the label gauge pieces to the sides of the base as shown in Fig. 27 with glue, panel pins and screws. Finish as in Chapter 1.

LABELLING & FILLING GAUGE

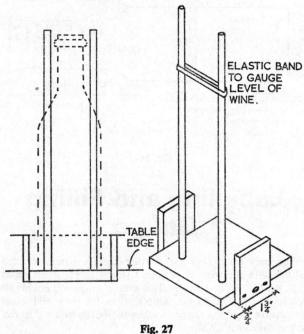

ELASTIC BAND TO GAUGE LEVEL OF WINE.

TABLE EDGE

$\frac{3}{4}$" $1\frac{3}{4}$"

Fig. 27

To use
Filling

Stand gauge with the dowels upright, place a bottle to be filled on the base, fill to the desired level, stretch an elastic band across the two dowels at the level of wine in the bottle, this gives the level for filling subsequent bottles.

Labelling

After filling and corking, lay the gauge on its back with the lip of the base overhanging the edge of the work-top. Lay a bottle on the dowels, mark the position required for the bottom edge of the label on the plywood side pieces, attach labels to the bottles using these marks.

Do not forget to place the label between the seams of the bottle. This will give a more professional finish.

Unit System Bottle Rack (Type 1)

This type of rack lends itself ideally to the unit system of bottle storage. When made as described, that is 7″ deep, the racks can be stood side by side on a shelf, worktop, etc. If they are to be stacked one on top of the other over two units high they must be made 9″ deep and additional support given in the form of glassplates or 1″ square battens fixed to the back edge of the units and then screwed to a firm wall.

Construction

Cramp the top, base and three shelves together, then as shown in Fig. 28, mark and drill the holes to accommodate the vertical dowels.

Mark the positions of the shelves on the inner surface of the sides and glue and pin the shelf supports in place, keeping them ½″ back from the front edge.

Glue and pin the top and base between the sides, apply glue to the shelf bearers and slide the shelves into position. Place the dowels into the holes whilst the shelves are pinned through the sides. Stand the unit upright, raise the dowels ¼″, apply glue to the dowels and lower into their final position. A ¾″ veneer pin driven through the front edges into the dowel will give added strength. Fit the 11″ bearer to the base, in front of the dowels, with glue and panel pins.

Check for squareness, then glue and pin the hardboard to the back edges of the top, base and sides.

Paint to choice as described in Chapter 1.

UNIT SYSTEM BOTTLE RACK

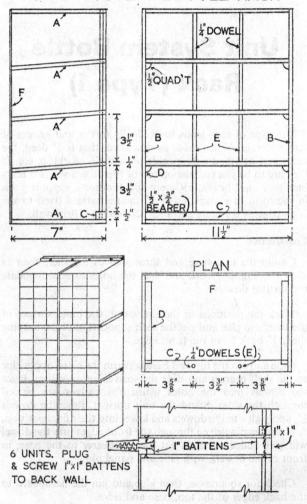

6 UNITS. PLUG
& SCREW I"xI" BATTENS
TO BACK WALL

Fig. 28

Cutting list

5 off $11'' \times 7'' \times \frac{1}{4}''$ / 279mm × 178mm × 6mm plywood. (Top, base and three shelves.) *A*.

2 off 1' $3\frac{3}{4}'' \times 7'' \times \frac{1}{4}''$ / 400mm × 178mm × 6mm plywood. (Sides.) *B*.

1 off $11'' \times \frac{1}{2}'' \times \frac{3}{4}''$ / 279mm × 13mm × 19mm. (Bearer.) *C*.

6 off $6'' \times \frac{1}{2}''$ / 152mm × 13mm quadrant or moulding. (Shelf supports.) *D*.

2 off 1' $3\frac{3}{4}'' \times \frac{1}{4}''$ / 400mm × 6mm dowel. (Bottle separators.) *E*.

1 off $11\frac{1}{2}'' \times 1' 3\frac{3}{4}''$ / 292mm × 400mm hardboard. (Back.) *F*.
Panel pins, hardboard pins and glue.

Tools required

Saw, plane, hammer, cramp, brace, $\frac{1}{4}''$ drill bit, rule, nail punch.

Bottle Rack (Type 2)

This is probably the easiest and quickest type of bottle rack to build, holding 88 bottles, 8 high (3') by 11 wide (3' 10").

Cutting list

2 off 2' $8'' \times 7'' \times 1''$ / 813mm × 178mm × 25mm. (Sides.)

1 off 3' $10'' \times 7'' \times 1''$ / 1m 168mm × 178mm × 25mm. (Top.)

1 off 3' $10'' \times 9'' \times 1''$ / 1m 168mm × 229mm × 25mm. (Base.)

8 off 3' $10'' \times \frac{3}{4}'' \times \frac{1}{2}''$ / 1m 168mm × 19mm × 13mm. (Front horizontal bearers.)

10 off 2' $9\frac{1}{2}'' \times \frac{1}{2}''$ / 851mm × 13mm half round moulding. (Vertical front supports.)

1 off $4' \times 3' \times \frac{1}{8}''$ / 1m 219mm × 914mm × 3mm hardboard, plywood, or other thin wood. Back.

3 off $10'' \times 2'' \times 1''$ / 254mm × 51mm × 25mm. (Feet.)

7 off 3' $10'' \times \frac{1}{2}'' \times \frac{1}{2}''$ / 1m 168mm × 13mm × 13mm. (Back horizontal bearers.)

77 off $7'' \times 3'' \times \frac{1}{8}''$ / 178mm × 76mm × 3mm.

BOTTLE RACK (TYPE 2)

PLAN

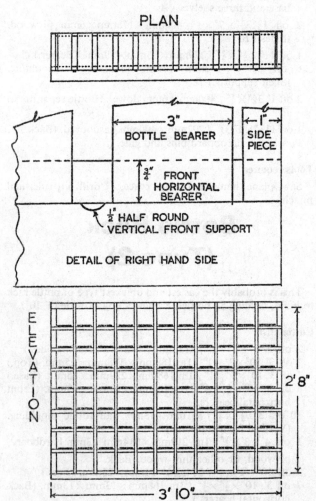

3"
BOTTLE BEARER

1"
SIDE PIECE

3/4"
FRONT HORIZONTAL BEARER

1/2" HALF ROUND VERTICAL FRONT SUPPORT

DETAIL OF RIGHT HAND SIDE

ELEVATION

2' 8"

3' 10"

Fig. 29

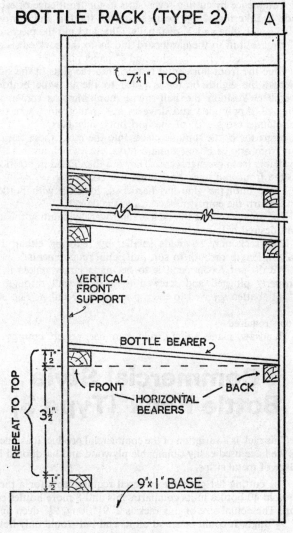

BOTTLE RACK (TYPE 2)

A

7"×1" TOP

VERTICAL
FRONT
SUPPORT

BOTTLE BEARER

REPEAT TO TOP

1½"

3½"

1½"

FRONT

HORIZONTAL
BEARERS

BACK

9"×1" BASE

Fig. 30

Commence by cutting seven slots in the front edge of each side to take the $\frac{3}{4}'' \times \frac{1}{2}''$ bearers, and fix the top and bottom pieces with glue and 2″ oval nails. Glue and pin the pieces of $\frac{1}{2}''$ square stuff to the hardboard and fix to the back edges of the assembled parts with glue and $\frac{3}{4}''$ panel pins.

Glue the front horizontal bearers into the slots in the side pieces; the eighth bearer is glued to the 9″ wide bottom member. Position the half-round mouldings, as shown in Fig. 29. Apply glue and drive in a $\frac{3}{4}''$ panel pin where the mouldings cross each of the horizontal members.

Insert the bottle support pieces into the rack; these can be cut from orange boxes, tomato trays, etc., which are readily available from greengrocers. They are then glued in position to the front and back horizontal bearers.

Leave until the glue has hardened, load up with bottles and return the empty milk crates to the dairy!

The appearance of the rack is improved by painting to suit any desired colour scheme.

This rack may be made smaller by reducing either the height, length or both to suit individual requirements.

We do not recommend it to be made larger unless it is properly plugged and screwed to a solid wall through a $1'' \times 1''$ batten screwed to the top member. Detail A, Fig. 30.

Tools required

Handsaw, plane, square, rule, hammer, punch, cramps.

Commercial Style Bottle Rack (Type 3)

This rack is a variation of the commercial product inasmuch as we have used easily obtainable plywood and hardboard in place of metal strips.

The cutting list gives the material requirements for a rack to hold 40 bottles in its compartments and 8 more bottles on top. The actual size of this rack is 2′ $9\frac{1}{2}''$ long, $9\frac{1}{8}''$ deep and 1′ $9\frac{1}{2}''$ high. It could be stood on its end but would only hold five bottles on the top, making a total of 45 bottles.

Bottle racks
Left Commercial type. *Right* Unit system rack

Rack to hold six bottles. Ideal for standing on sideboard or bar top

Above Fermentation cupboard to keep eight gallons of wine at 70° F. *Below* Bottle draining stand

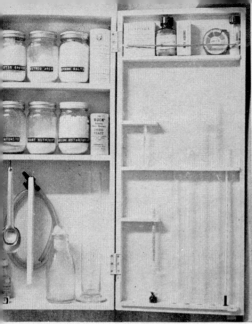

Cabinet to keep all small pieces of equipment together and ready to hand

The easy way to dispense wine from a half-gallon jar

Bottle carrier for easy transportation

A tidy way of crushing malt grain

Cutting list

54 off 9″ × 1″ × 1″ / 229mm × 26mm × 26mm sawn. (Bottle rests.)

9 off 1′ 9½″ × 1″ × ⅛″ / 546mm × 26mm × 3mm plywood. (Horizontals.)

6 off 2′ 9½″ × 1″ × ⅛″ / 851mm × 26mm × 3mm plywood. (Verticals.)

1 off 1′ 9½″ × 2′ 9½″ × ⅛″ / 546mm × 851mm × 3mm hard-board. (Back.)

1½″ / 38mm roundhead wire nails.

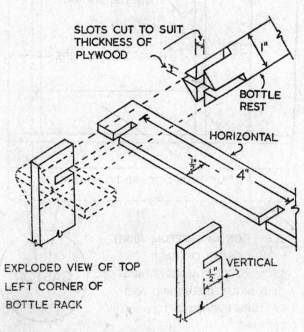

SLOTS CUT TO SUIT THICKNESS OF PLYWOOD

BOTTLE REST

HORIZONTAL

4″

EXPLODED VIEW OF TOP LEFT CORNER OF BOTTLE RACK

VERTICAL

Fig. 31

BOTTLE RACK (TYPE 3)

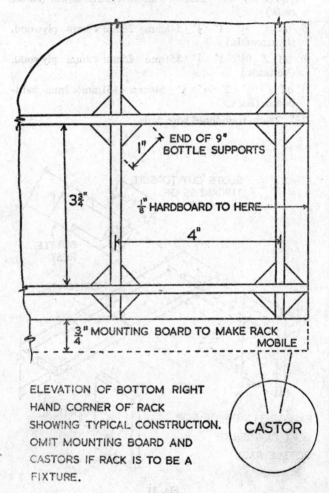

1"

END OF 9"
BOTTLE SUPPORTS

$\frac{1}{8}$" HARDBOARD TO HERE

$3\frac{3}{4}$"

4"

$\frac{3}{4}$" MOUNTING BOARD TO MAKE RACK
MOBILE

ELEVATION OF BOTTOM RIGHT
HAND CORNER OF RACK
SHOWING TYPICAL CONSTRUCTION.
OMIT MOUNTING BOARD AND
CASTORS IF RACK IS TO BE A
FIXTURE.

CASTOR

Fig. 32

45 BOTTLE RACK

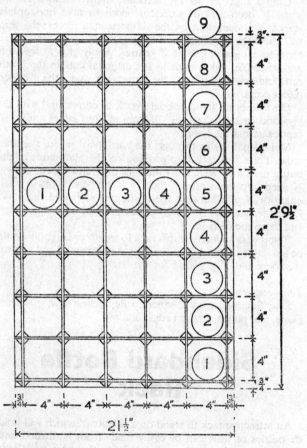

Fig. 33

Construction

Having cut all the pieces to size and cleaned up all rough edges, cut slots 1" deep in one end of the bottle rests, wide enough to take the plywood strips, Fig. 31.

Cramp together all the verticals, mark out and cut six slots, $\frac{1}{2}$" deep and of sufficient width to take horizontals. Repeat this operation on the six horizontal pieces; the slots will allow the horizontal and vertical pieces to be interlocked, forming compartments at 4" centres. Apply glue to the slots and assemble. Apply glue to the diagonal cuts in the bottle rests and drive them on to the framework where the plywood pieces cross.

Draw lines on the hardboard back to correspond with the plywood centres, that is $\frac{3}{4}$" in from all four edges and at 4" centres across the board.

Make small holes through the hardboard where the lines cross. Place the back into position on the plain ends of the bottle rests and drive nails through the holes approximately $\frac{1}{4}$" deep into the centre of the 1"×1" timbers. Work a small quantity of glue between the bottle rest ends and the back. Place the assembly on a flat surface with the back uppermost and drive the nails in.

If you wish to increase this rack in length or height it would be advisable to use $\frac{3}{16}$" plywood for the horizontal and vertical members and $\frac{1}{4}$" plywood for the back.

Tools required

Saw, hammer, cramp, square, rule, coping saw, $\frac{1}{4}$" chisel, plane, nail punch, straight edge, bradawl.

Sideboard Bottle Rack

An attractive rack to stand on a sideboard which will hold six bottles of wine can be easily made from hardwood and dowelling. A dark coloured wood for the rests and light coloured dowels look very effective when polished. Softwood can be used if a painted finish is required.

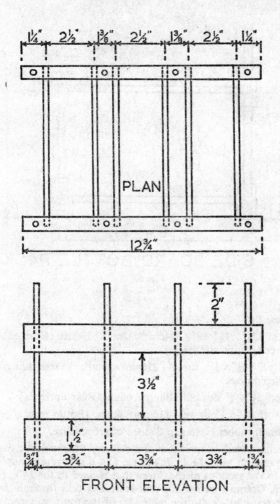

PLAN

FRONT ELEVATION

SIDE BOARD BOTTLE RACK

Fig. 34

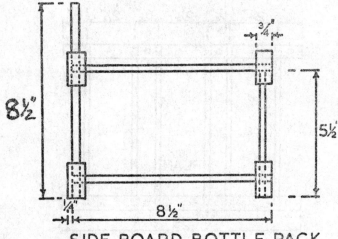

SIDE BOARD BOTTLE RACK
Fig. 35

Cutting list

4 off $12\frac{3}{4}'' \times 1\frac{1}{2}'' \times \frac{3}{4}''$ / 324mm × 38mm × 19mm. (Horizontal rests, front and back.)

4 off $8\frac{1}{2}'' \times \frac{1}{4}''$ dowel / 216mm × 6mm. (Front upright separators.)

4 off $5\frac{1}{2}'' \times \frac{1}{4}''$ dowel / 140mm × 6mm. (Rear uprights.)

12 off $8\frac{1}{2}'' \times \frac{1}{4}''$ dowel / 216mm × 6mm. (Bottle rests.)

4 small rubber buffers or 2 strips of green baize.

Cramp together, mark out and drill right through the two front rests to take the $\frac{1}{4}''$ dowelling. Cut a groove and apply glue to the sections of the dowel that is fixed in the $1\frac{1}{2}'' \times \frac{3}{4}''$ pieces. Cramp together the rear rests and drill through the lower rest and $\frac{1}{2}''$ into the underside of the top rest. Groove and glue the $5\frac{1}{2}''$ lengths of dowel into position. Place the front assembly onto the bench and cramp the back section on to it. Mark and drill through the back frame and $\frac{1}{2}''$ into the front pieces. Cut grooves in the ends of the dowel and

68

glue into position. Clean off all surplus glue while it is still wet. Rub down all the rough edges and the top of the four front separators with glasspaper and varnish or paint to choice. Fix the rubber buffers or baize into place.

Tools required

Cramp, rule, brace, $\frac{1}{4}''$ bit, saw, plane, chisel, trysquare screwdriver, hammer and bradawl.

Half-Gallon Jar Dispenser

If you are accustomed to serving wine direct from a half gallon jar this novel dispenser will be found to be invaluable. It is made in two parts, the base and side supports and the jar cradle, pivoted on two pieces of dowel. Commence by cutting the side supports as shown in Fig. 36 and nail them with $1\frac{1}{2}''$ ovals to the ends of the base. Punch the nail heads well below the surface.

The cradle consists of seven components, a base, being the centre waste piece from the jar retaining ring, a cradle, front and back, L-shaped pieces and two dowel pivots.

Having cut the pieces to the sizes given, glasspaper all rough edges. Glue and pin the base in position at the bottom and the retaining ring to the top edges of the cradle. Glue and pin the L-shaped pieces to the underside of the base ensuring they are at 90° to the cradle. Drill the $\frac{1}{4}''$ holes through the cradle ends and glue the dowels in position. When drilling the hole to take the dowel pivot, place the top edge of the cradle in the jaws of a vice to prevent the plywood from splitting. Fix a rubber buffer to each corner of the base or alternatively glue baize to the base to prevent scratching of polished surfaces.

Do not place a jar in the completed dispenser until the glue has thoroughly hardened. It may be finished by painting or varnishing with polyurethane to choice.

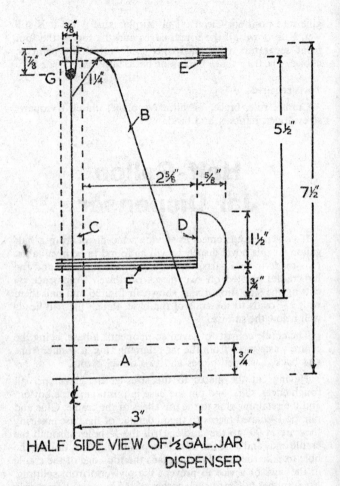

HALF SIDE VIEW OF ½ GAL. JAR
DISPENSER

Fig. 36

HALF GALLON JAR DISPENSER

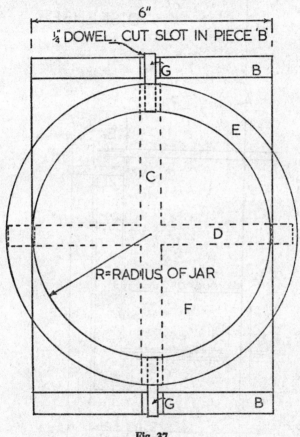

Fig. 37

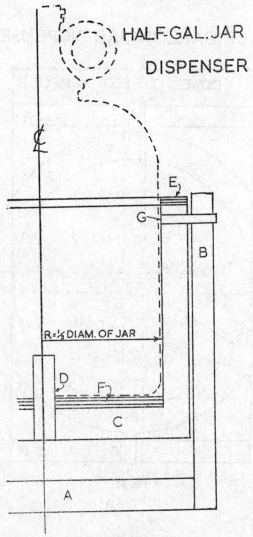

HALF-GAL. JAR
DISPENSER

R = ½ DIAM. OF JAR

Fig. 38

72

Cutting list

1 off $7\frac{1}{2}'' \times 6'' \times \frac{3}{4}''$ / 191mm × 152mm × 19mm plywood or blockboard. (Base.) *A*.

2 off $7\frac{1}{2}'' \times 6'' \times \frac{1}{2}''$ / 191mm × 152mm × 13mm plywood. (Side supports cut to shape.) *B*.

1 off $7\frac{1}{4}'' \times 5\frac{1}{2}'' \times \frac{1}{2}''$ / 184mm × 133mm × 13mm plywood. (Cradle.) *C*.

2 off $3\frac{1}{4}'' \times 2\frac{1}{2}'' \times \frac{1}{2}''$ / 83mm × 64mm × 13mm plywood. (L-shaped pieces cut from cradlewaste.) *D*.

1 off $7\frac{1}{4}''$ / 184mm diameter, $\frac{1}{2}''$ / 6mm plywood. (Jar retaining ring.) *E*.

1 off $5\frac{5}{16}''$ / 151mm diameter, $\frac{1}{4}''$ / 6mm plywood. (Cradle base from centre of jar retaining ring.) *F*.

2 off $1\frac{1}{4}''$ / 32mm lengths of $\frac{1}{4}''$ / 6mm dowel, glue, panel pins, $1\frac{1}{2}''$ oval nails.

4 small rubber buffers or green baize $8\frac{1}{2}'' \times 6''$ / 216mm × 152mm.

Tools required

Compass, rule, handsaw, coping saw, hammer, punch, drill, drill bits, vice or small cramps, bradawl, screwdriver, square.

1-Gallon Jar Dispenser

This dispenser is basically the same as the $\frac{1}{2}$-gallon size. You will notice from the cutting list and Fig. 39 that most timber thicknesses have been increased and obviously larger dimensions are given to accommodate the 1 gallon jar.

ONE GALLON JAR DISPENSER

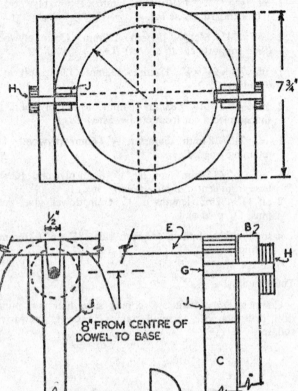

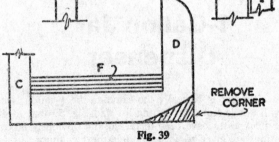

H

J

7¾"

½"

E

B

H

G

J

C

8" FROM CENTRE OF
DOWEL TO BASE

D

F

C

REMOVE
CORNER

Fig. 39

Cutting list

1 off $9'' \times 7\frac{3}{4}'' \times \frac{3}{4}''$ / 229mm $\times$ 197mm $\times$ 19mm plywood or blockboard. (Base.) *A*.

2 off $9\frac{1}{2}'' \times 7\frac{3}{4}'' \times \frac{1}{2}''$ / 241mm $\times$ 197mm $\times$ 13mm plywood. (Side supports cut to shape.) *B*.

1 off $8\frac{1}{2}'' \times 7\frac{5}{8}'' \times \frac{3}{4}''$ / 216mm $\times$ 194mm $\times$ 19mm plywood. (Cradle.) *C*.

2 off $4'' \times 3'' \times \frac{3}{4}''$ / 102mm $\times$ 76mm $\times$ 19mm plywood. (L-shaped pieces cut from cradle waste.) *D*.

1 off $8\frac{1}{2}''$ / 216mm diameter $\frac{3}{8}''$ / 10mm plywood. (Jar retaining ring.) *E*.

1 off $7\frac{1}{2}''$ / 191mm diameter $\frac{3}{8}''$ / 10mm plywood. (Cradle base from centre of jar retaining ring.) *F*.

4 off $1\frac{3}{4}'' \times \frac{3}{4}''$ / 44mm $\times$ 19mm, $\frac{3}{8}''$ / 10mm or $\frac{1}{2}''$ / 13mm plywood. (Cradle strengtheners.) *J*.

2 off $1\frac{1}{8}''$ / 29mm diameter $\frac{3}{8}''$ / 10mm plywood. (Dowel discs.) *H*.

2 off $2\frac{1}{4}''$ / 44mm lengths of $\frac{3}{8}''$ / 10mm dowel, glue, panel pins, $1\frac{1}{2}''$ / 38mm oval nails, 4 small rubber buffers or green baize ($10'' \times 8''$ / 254mm $\times$ 203mm).

Assembly is the same as given for the $\frac{1}{2}$ gallon dispenser. The only variations are the addition of strengtheners that are fitted (glued and pinned) to the pivot ends of the cradle prior to drilling the holes for the dowels. The plywood discs are drilled and then glued to the ends of the dowels to keep the cradle central when in use.

Tools required

Compass, rule, handsaw, coping saw, hammer, punch, drill, drill bits, vice or small cramps, bradawl, screwdriver, square.

Mobile Bar

A bar such as the one described here would fit into almost any home, with the advantages of being portable, inexpensive and easy to construct. Due to the infinite combination of finishes currently available, we have left the choice to the constructor. The bar top, which gets a lot of wear, should be covered with a sheet of glass or laminated plastic to give an attractive, easily cleaned surface.

Cutting list

$\frac{3}{4}$" / 19mm blockboard, chipboard, plywood, etc.

1 off 1' 5$\frac{1}{2}$" × 3' 10$\frac{1}{2}$" / 445mm × 1m 181mm.
(Lower front.) B.

2 off 1' 5$\frac{3}{4}$" × 3' 10$\frac{1}{2}$" / 451mm × 1m 181mm.
(Top and base.) C.

1 off 1' 3" × 3' 10$\frac{1}{2}$". / 381mm × 1m 181mm. (Top shelf.) D.

1 off 1' 5" × 3' 10$\frac{1}{2}$" / 432mm × 1m 181mm.
(Middle shelf.) E.

1 off 6" × 3' 10$\frac{1}{2}$" / 152mm × 1m. 181mm. (Glasses shelf.) F.

2 off 1' 5$\frac{3}{4}$" × 3' 2" / 451mm × 952mm. (End pieces.) A1.

2 off 3' $\frac{1}{2}$" × 5$\frac{1}{4}$" / 927mm × 133mm. (Back ends.) B1.

4 off 3' $\frac{1}{2}$" × 9" / 927mm × 229mm. (Doors.) C1.

1 off 1' 1$\frac{1}{2}$" × 1' $\frac{3}{4}$" / 343mm × 324mm. (Division.) D1.

1 off 1' 5$\frac{3}{4}$" × 1' $\frac{1}{4}$" / 451mm × 400mm. (Division.) D2.

1 off 6" × 4' / 152mm × 1m 219mm. (Front retainer.) E1.

1 off 2' 1$\frac{1}{4}$" × 4' × $\frac{1}{4}$" / 642mm × 1m 219mm × 6mm.
(Front.) A.

14 ft. of $\frac{1}{2}$" quadrant / 4m 268mm × 13mm.

Glue, 1$\frac{1}{2}$" × 8 gauge countersunk woodscrews, $\frac{3}{4}$" panel pins, 8 pairs of 2$\frac{1}{2}$" hinges and screws, 3 4" necked shootbolts with plates and screws, 1 set of plate fixing castors, 2 cupboard catches and handle or cupboard lock. See Chapter 5 for details of bottle rack construction.

Construction

Commence by gluing and screwing the lower front (B) to the middle shelf (E) and base (C). These pieces should then fixed between the two ends (A1). Fix the divisions D1 and D2

PORTABLE BAR

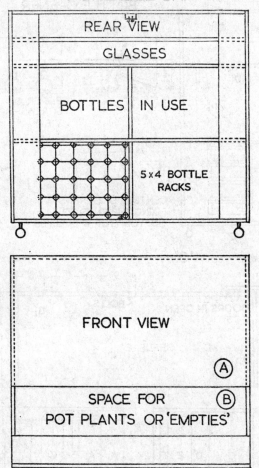

REAR VIEW

GLASSES

BOTTLES | IN USE

5 x 4 BOTTLE RACKS

FRONT VIEW

Ⓐ

SPACE FOR Ⓑ
POT PLANTS OR 'EMPTIES'

Fig. 40

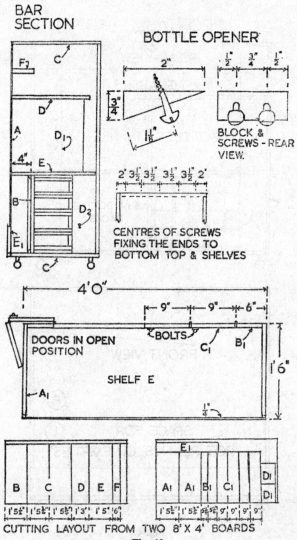

BAR SECTION

BOTTLE OPENER

2"

3/4"

1⅛"

½" 3/4" ½"

BLOCK & SCREWS - REAR VIEW.

2' 3½' 3½' 3½' 3½' 2'

CENTRES OF SCREWS FIXING THE ENDS TO BOTTOM TOP & SHELVES

4'0"

9" 9" 6"

DOORS IN OPEN POSITION

BOLTS

C₁

B₁

SHELF E

A₁

1'6"

¼"

CUTTING LAYOUT FROM TWO 8' X 4' BOARDS

B C D E F

1'5½" 1'5½" 1'5½" 1'3" 1'5" 6"

E₁

A₁ A₁ B₁ C₁ D₁ D₁

1'5½" 1'5½" 5½" 5½" 9" 9" 9" 9"

Fig. 41

into position, then glue and screw the top shelf (D), the glasses shelf (F) and the bar top (C) into place.

After checking that the carcase is square, glue and pin the front (A) on to the edges of the top, shelves and division. The front retaining piece (E) is glued and screwed to the base and sides after fixing the ½" quadrant as shown in bar section, Fig. 41. Pieces of plywood ¾" wide are then attached to the edge of pieces (A1) between the front and the front retainer (E1). The back end pieces (B1) which must be a tight fit between the top and base, are glued in position and the doors hung in "pairs" from them. The bolts are fitted to the outer doors and to one of the centre doors. Fix the cupboard catches and handle (lock) to the remaining door. Screw the castors to the base approximately 1" from the edges of each corner.

If a commercial bottle opener is not available one can be simply constructed from a piece of hardwood and two screws as shown in Fig. 41.

Finishes

Before ordering any materials, decide what the final finish of the bar should be. This is used as a guide to the quality of the timber required, i.e. if it is to be covered with laminated plastic a cheap grade plywood could be used whereas a painted finish would need a good quality plywood or block-board to give satisfactory results without too much filling and rubbing down.

Some of the alternative finishes could be:
> self adhesive plastic sheet,
> vinyl floor or wall covering,
> artificial stone in plastic sheet form,
> reeded hardboard,
> quilted plastic sheet, etc.,

to match or even contrast with the surrounding décor.

CHAPTER 6

Shed Winery

Everyone will have their own ideas about the size of a shed to suit their needs and the size we describe will be found to be adequate for the average winemaker.

We have inspected many commercially made sheds and have come to the conclusion that if they are to be used as a winery they must be considered as a protection against the elements only. They are not constructed to take the comparatively heavy loads of liquid and glass the winemaker would want to store in them. Therefore, all the racks, shelves, etc., must be self-supporting and on a firm base. The floors supplied by some manufacturers with the sheds are not needed, but some sort of duck boarding between the racks is desirable as concrete can be very cold to the feet.

The roof and side walls must be insulated to afford protection against the variable temperatures encountered in this country. Ventilation is needed and "hit and miss" ventilators should be installed at high level to help control temperatures. A work surface, about 4 ft. long and situated below the windows, is necessary. The windows should be double glazed, the door and the opening parts of the windows treated with foam draught excluder strip.

The siting of the winery is important and is discussed later in the chapter. A good path from the house to the winery is an asset especially when weather conditions are bad.

Electricity for heating and lighting is needed and a water supply could be run to the shed via a permanent pipe below ground or a temporary plastic hose connected to the kitchen tap, although this would require emptying after use owing to the risk of contamination. A water supply is not essential; we have always carried water as required in plastic buckets.

Our proposed layout is for a shed 8' long by 6' wide. All racks and shelves are self-supporting, although temporary supports to the vertical members of the shed are allowed during construction.

These supports should be removed before the racks etc. are used. We have allowed sufficient storage space for some 250 to 300 bottles of wine, but this may be varied to suit individual requirements.

The majority of winemakers use one gallon jars for fermentation and storage, therefore the shelving is designed accordingly and will accommodate at least 80 jars. Racks for small barrels or ex wine 5's could be placed along one wall, but it is left to personal choice.

SITING THE SHED WINERY
Selecting the site

Ideally a winery shed should be sited in a cool place, in the shade of a tree, or on the north side of a wall or house, being the most suitable position as the shade provided helps to keep the interior cool during the summer months.

Excavating for the base

Having selected the site, peg out the shape to the dimensions of the base of the shed. Dig out the soil approximately 9in. deep over the whole area. Remove the surplus top soil to another part of the garden. Make sure the bottom of the excavation is level and clear off all loose soil. Fill the hole with hardcore to a depth of 5 in., well packed and rammed down, cover the hardcore with sand, ash or other fine material such as crushed brick mortar, crushed broken breeze blocks, etc. The fine material should be well soaked with water from a watering can or hosepipe to wash it into the crevices between the larger pieces of hardcore to make a firmer base.

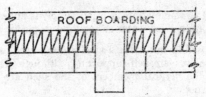

SECTION THROUGH PURLIN
SHOWING INSULATION AND
FIXING BEADS

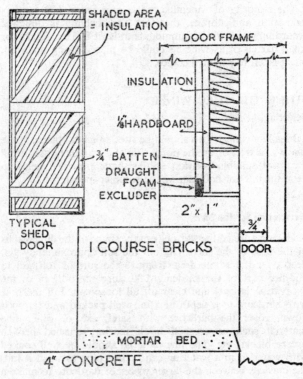

SHADED AREA
= INSULATION

DOOR FRAME

INSULATION

⅛" HARDBOARD

¾" BATTEN

DRAUGHT
FOAM
EXCLUDER

2" x 1"

¾"

DOOR

TYPICAL
SHED
DOOR

I COURSE BRICKS

MORTAR BED

4" CONCRETE

Fig. 42

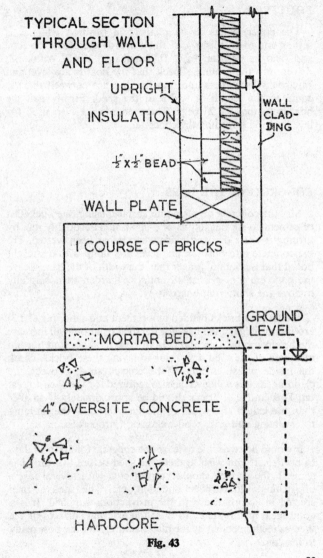

TYPICAL SECTION
THROUGH WALL
AND FLOOR

UPRIGHT

INSULATION

WALL CLADDING

$\frac{1}{2}" \times \frac{1}{2}"$ BEAD

WALL PLATE

1 COURSE OF BRICKS

GROUND LEVEL

MORTAR BED

4" OVERSITE CONCRETE

HARDCORE

Fig. 43

SHUTTERING

The concrete has to be retained in position while it is setting and to do this 4″ × 1″ thick boards are placed on edge and held in position by 2 ft. lengths of 2″ × 2″ softwood, driven into the ground. Check that the boards are level and square at the corners and that the distance between them is equal to the length or width of the shed. Firmly nail the boards to the 2″ × 2″ pegs. These boards are also used for levelling and screeding the concrete.

CONCRETING THE BASE

Mix the concrete on a smooth surface, using one bucketful of cement to six bucketfuls of ¾″ ballast. Thoroughly mix by turning it twice dry and twice when it has been wetted. Tip the concrete into position and level and tamp with a straight board that is about 6″ longer than the width of the base. Leave the concrete for at least 48 hours to harden then carefully remove the shuttering boards.

A course of bricks bedded in a cement and sand mix (1 : 3) around the edge of the base for the shed to sit on, will increase the headroom by 3 in. and help to keep the floor and bottom members of the shed dry. Prior to laying these bricks, check the inside measurements of the erected shed, between the cladding, as this will give the size required for the shed to rest on. This course of bricks should be approximately ½″ smaller than the length and width of the shed to allow the cladding to overhang and give good weathering properties.

It would be advisable to leave the concrete for 10 to 14 days to harden. If you wish to erect the shed before this time has elapsed, the surface should be protected with several layers of sacking, old carpets, underfelt, etc. The shed is then erected in accordance with the instructions supplied. It is a good idea, at this stage, to treat the external surfaces of the shed as recommended by the manufacturer. We are now ready to insulate.

INSULATION

Timber is a good insulator but not sufficient for our purposes. Therefore all the inside surfaces of the winery must have some sort of added insulation to help keep the temperature down in the warmer months and up during the cooler months.

We have successfully used $\frac{3}{4}''$ thick expanded polystyrene boards to do this. The polystyrene is cut with a knife or saw to fit in between the vertical and horizontal members, and is held in position with either lengths of softwood or can be glued with heavy duty paste or polystyrene adhesive if the internal surface of the cladding is flat. The underside of the timber roof may be treated as for walls, but if constructed from corrugated plastic or asbestos, some extra purlins must be added to give a fixing for the polystyrene and prevent sagging. (See Fig. 49.)

The door is insulated by gluing and screwing lengths of softwood to its top, bottom and both edges, far enough in to just clear the stops on the door frame. Cut polystyrene to fit between the softwood battens and hold in position with a sheet of $\frac{1}{8}''$ thick hardboard glued and pinned to the edges. Some sheds will require a $2'' \times 1''$ hardwood strip, the width of the door, fixed across the threshold to act as a stop and help prevent draughts. Fit foam draught excluder strips around the door. (See Fig. 42.)

Polystyrene can be painted, but to effect a superior finish it can be covered with pieces of hardboard held in position with small quadrant or the timber fillets if used.

Windows can be the cause of a lot of heat loss and solar gain and they should be double glazed with 24 oz. clear sheet glass cut $\frac{3}{8}''$ larger than the window frame and held in position with rebated halfround softwood strips glued and pinned to the sash. Make sure the inside surfaces of the glass are spotlessly clean before fixing as the glass cannot be cleaned afterwards. This double glazing work should only be carried out on a dry warm day to prevent moist air being trapped between the panes and showing as condensation when the temperature changes. Fit foam draught excluder strip to the edges of opening windows. (See Fig. 44.)

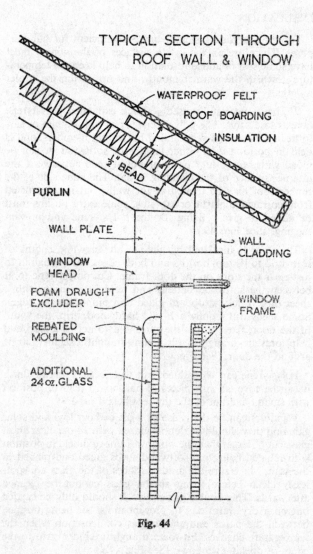

TYPICAL SECTION THROUGH
ROOF WALL & WINDOW

WATERPROOF FELT

ROOF BOARDING

INSULATION

½" BEAD

PURLIN

WALL PLATE

WALL CLADDING

WINDOW HEAD

FOAM DRAUGHT EXCLUDER

WINDOW FRAME

REBATED MOULDING

ADDITIONAL 24 oz. GLASS

Fig. 44

86

All that remains now is to make good the joints between the bricks and the walls with a 3 : 1 sand and cement mixture, and to cut two 9″ × 3″ holes in the end sections and 11″ × 5″ holes in the polystyrene sheets. A 1″ × 1″ batten is screwed around the opening on the inside and 9″ × 3″ "hit and miss" type ventilators screwed to the battens and metal shields fitted to the outside to make the holes weatherproof. (See Fig. 45.)

ELECTRICITY

Lighting and heating are necessary and electricity will be found to be most convenient and a satisfactory method to use. Paraffin should not be used for heating as there is a risk of contaminating the brew; also the normal grade of expanded polystyrene is inflammable.

A lighting point and two 13 amp. power points will cover most needs in the winery. A qualified electrician should be employed to carry out this work. A D.I.Y. kit is available for an electrical installation in a garage or shed and this can be used in the winery. It is advisable, in the interest of safety, to have this work tested by the local electrical authority.

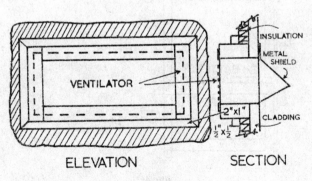

Fig. 45

With all windows and doors sealed off and with the insulation to the roof and walls, there should be no air change/heat loss except when the door and the ventilators are opened. The most suitable form of heating is by greenhouse-tubular heater and by using the following calculations it is easy to arrive at the heating requirements.

BENCH

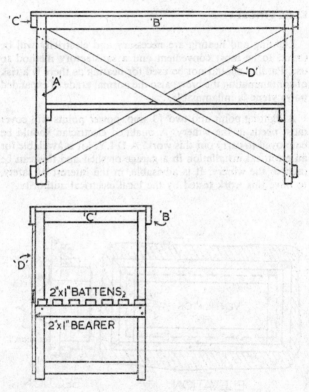

Fig. 46

Volume of shed: $8' \times 6' \times 6' = 288$ cu. ft.

Power requirement (to 60° F.) = 1.5 watts per cu. ft.

Therefore total heat loss × power requirement is:

$$288 \times 1.5 = 432 \text{ watts.}$$

Greenhouse-tubular heaters come in two basic wattage ratings and to find the footage of heaters required would be 432 divided by 80 or 60 watts (80 or 60 being the foot run rating of the heaters).

$$432/80 = 5.4 \text{ ft. or } 432/60 = 7.2 \text{ ft.}$$

We suggest that two heaters, 3 ft. at 80 watts per ft. rating or two at 4 ft. at 60 watts per ft. rating, are used to start with in conjunction with an airtype thermostat. The heaters should be mounted clear off the floor and with about 3 ft. distance between them and controlled by a five amp thermostat mounted about 3 ft. from the floor.

A bench or table, $4' \times 1' \, 8''$, is an ideal size to fit into the winery and gives ample room for the bottling, labelling operations, etc.

Cutting list

4 off $2' \, 5\frac{1}{4}'' \times 1\frac{1}{2}'' \times 1\frac{1}{2}''$ / 743mm × 38mm × 38mm. (Legs.) *A*.

2 off $4' \times 3'' \times 1''$ / 1m 219mm × 36mm × 25mm. (Front and back rails.) *B*.

4 off $1' \, 8'' \times 2'' \times 1''$ / 508mm × 51mm × 25mm. (End rails.) *C*.

2 off $4' \, 9'' \times 2'' \times \frac{3}{4}''$ / 1m 448mm × 51mm × 19mm. (Cross braces cut to shape.) *D*.

1 off $4' \times 1' \, 8'' \times \frac{3}{4}''$ / 1m 219mm × 508mm × 19mm blockboard or chipboard.

1 off $4' \times 1' \, 10''$ / 1m 219mm × 559mm laminated plastic sheet.

42 $2'' \times 8$ gauge countersunk woodscrews.

6 $1\frac{1}{2}''$ / 38mm × 8 gauge countersunk woodscrews. (Fixing for top to end rails.)

Glue and screw the end rails (*C*) to the face of the legs (*A*). The top rails are kept flush with the ends of the legs and the other two rails are fixed 1in. up from the bottom of the legs. (See Fig. 46.) With the end rails facing outwards glue and screw the top on to the rails, keeping the rails flush with the corners of the top. The front and back rails are glued and screwed to the edge of the top and on to the legs. This will cover the ragged edge of the blockboard. The cross braces are glued and screwed diagonally to the back legs. Fix the laminated plastic sheet with impact adhesive. The bench may be painted or varnished to choice as described in Chapter 1.

If shelf bearers are screwed to the inside faces of the legs about 1' 1" below the top end rails, a useful shelf can be fitted to take empty one gallon jars, bottles, etc. Alternatively the space under the bench could be used to house five or ten gallon carboys, wheeled into place on the trolleys described in Chapter 3.

A filter and racking stand, as described in Chapter 4 is fitted to a 3' × 11" piece of plywood or blockboard at least $\frac{1}{2}$" thick which is mounted on two pieces of 2" × $\frac{3}{4}$" softwood long enough to be screwed to the uprights of the shed. The fermentation cupboard is fixed on to a 2" × 1" piece of timber screwed to its top and to the shed uprights. Two legs, 2" × 1" in section, are screwed to the sides near the doors and rest on the floor to take the weight.

To construct a rack for storing the one-gallon jars along one side of the shed, you will need to make five frames as shown in Fig. 50. These are then spaced equidistantly and 3" in from the ends of the shed. The back bracing pieces are screwed into position to give rigidity and the front and back shelving slats are notched to take the 2" × 2" standards and glued and screwed in place. The whole rack is moved into its final position and then plugged and screwed to the floor. The remaining slats are spaced out and glued and screwed to the shelf bearers.

The coolest part of the winery is used to store bottled wine and racks, as described in Chapter 5, are constructed 8 bottles high by 5 bottles wide. This will give 180 bottles storage, i.e. 4 racks each holding 45 bottles. If more storage is required similar racks can be mounted on 1' 10" lengths of 9" × 1" softwood and a castor fitted at each corner to enable the rack to be easily moved and give access to the rear racks. (See Fig. 47.)

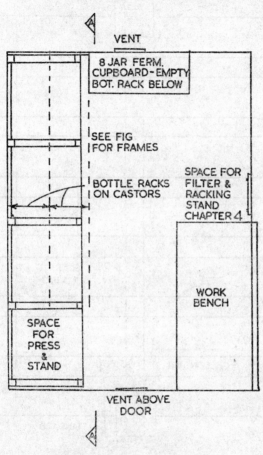

VENT

8 JAR FERM.
CUPBOARD–EMPTY
BOT. RACK BELOW

SEE FIG
FOR FRAMES

BOTTLE RACKS
ON CASTORS

SPACE FOR
FILTER &
RACKING
STAND
CHAPTER 4

WORK
BENCH

SPACE
FOR
PRESS
&
STAND

VENT ABOVE
DOOR

SUGGESTED LAYOUT
OF SHED WINERY

Fig. 47

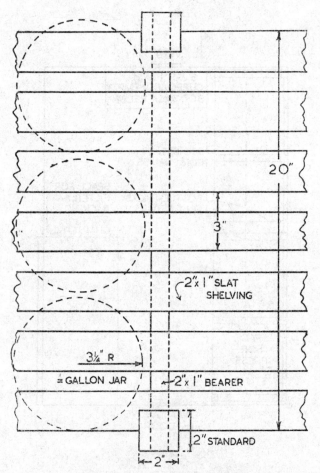

20"

3"

2" x 1" SLAT
SHELVING

3¼" R

= GALLON JAR

2" x 1" BEARER

2" STANDARD

2"

LAYOUT OF SLAT SHELVING NOTCH FRONT
& BACK SLATS AROUND STANDARDS

Fig. 48

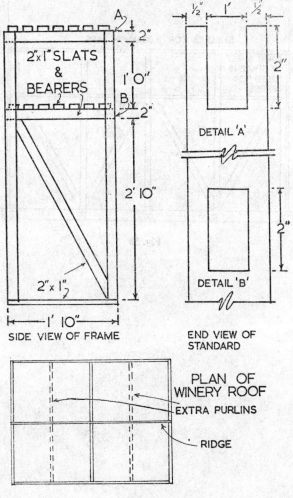

A

2"x1" SLATS
&
BEARERS

B

2"

1' 0"

2"

2' 10"

2"x1"

1' 10"

SIDE VIEW OF FRAME

½" 1" ½"

2"

DETAIL 'A'

2"

DETAIL 'B'

END VIEW OF
STANDARD

PLAN OF
WINERY ROOF

EXTRA PURLINS

RIDGE

Fig. 49

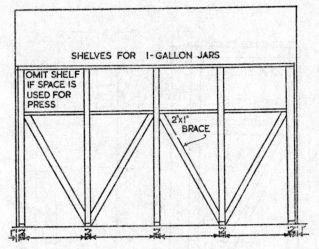

Fig. 50

Storage Cabinet for Small Items

This cabinet is designed to hold the majority of small items of equipment, most of the chemicals and yeasts used in the winery. It is basically constructed from $\frac{3}{8}"$ thick plywood and $\frac{1}{8}"$ hardboard.

Cutting list

All the following pieces are cut from $\frac{3}{8}"$ / 10mm plywood.
2 off $21\frac{3}{4}" \times 4\frac{1}{2}"$ / 552mm × 114mm. (Sides.)
2 off $10" \times 4\frac{1}{2}"$ / 254mm × 114mm. (Top and base.)
2 off $9\frac{1}{4}" \times 3\frac{1}{2}"$ / 235mm × 89mm. (Shelves.)
3 off $9\frac{1}{4}" \times 1"$ / 235mm × 25mm. (Ledges inside door.)
2 off $3" \times 1"$ / 57mm × 25mm. (Hydrometer and Vinometer.)
1 off $6" \times 2\frac{1}{2}"$ / 152mm × 64mm. (Support. Siphon tubing bracket, cut to shape.)
1 off $2" \times \frac{3}{4}"$ / 51mm × 19mm. (Door pull.)
2 screweyes.
1 pair $1\frac{1}{2}"$ / 38mm hinges and screws.
$\frac{3}{4}"$ / 19mm panel pins, wood glue.
2 keyhole glassplates and screws.
Magnetic cupboard catch.
2 pieces of $\frac{1}{8}"$ / 3mm hardboard $22\frac{1}{2}" \times 10\frac{1}{4}"$ / 571mm × 260mm. (Front and back.)

Construction

Glue and pin the top and base to the sides as shown in Fig. 52. The hardboard pieces are then glued and pinned to the front and back of the assembly. When the glue has hardened, draw a line $1\frac{1}{8}"$ from the front of the cabinet along the top, sides, and base. Saw the box in two along the lines drawn. The smaller section forms the opening door and the sawn edges should be planed and glasspapered smooth.

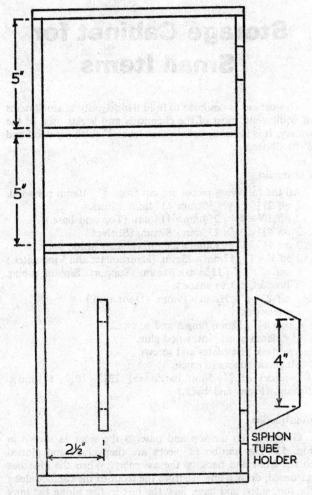

Fig. 51

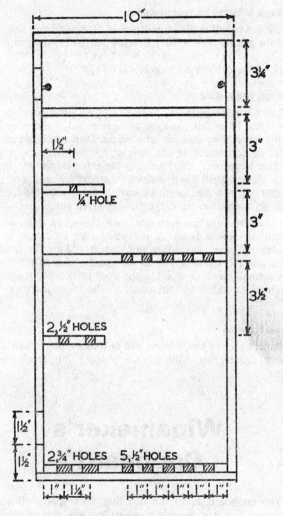

Fig. 52

Fittings in larger portion of cabinet

The first shelf is glued and pinned 5″ down from the top and the second shelf is fixed 5″ below the first. Cut the siphon tubing bracket to the shape shown. Glue and pin through the back of the cabinet into the bracket.

Fittings inside door

The centre ledge is then marked out with the positions of the holes. Place this piece on the bottom ledge and bore the $\frac{1}{2}$″ diameter holes through both pieces. Drill two $\frac{3}{4}$″ diameter holes to accommodate the base of the hydrometers in the bottom ledge only. Glue and pin the three ledges into positions shown. Drill the hydrometer support and glue and pin in place to suit the length of your hydrometers. Drill, glue and pin the vinometer support to the front and side.

Fix a screw-eye into each side piece, 1″ above the top ledge, fasten an elastic band to the screw-eyes to retain small packets of yeast, etc. Mark out, cut in and fix the hinges. Glue and pin the door-pull to the opening side of the door. Fix a small block of wood to the door to take the magnetic catch plate and screw the catch to the inside edge of the cabinet.

Tools required

Panel or tenon saw, coping, pad or fretsaw, plane, hammer, punch, square, rule, drill, or brace, $\frac{1}{2}$″ and $\frac{3}{4}$″ bits, screwdriver, chisel.

Winemaker's Cupboard

This cupboard, taking up very little floor space, will store 18 one-gallon jars, ferment 6 one-gallon jars, and afford two drawers to hold all the odd pieces of equipment, yeasts nutrients, etc.

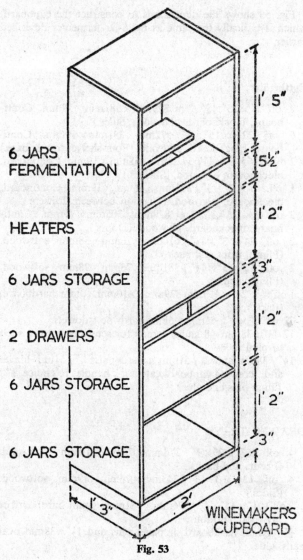

6 JARS FERMENTATION

HEATERS

6 JARS STORAGE

2 DRAWERS

6 JARS STORAGE

6 JARS STORAGE

1' 5"

5½"

1' 2"

3"

1' 2"

1' 2"

3"

1' 3"

2'

WINEMAKERS CUPBOARD

Fig. 53

99

Fig. 53 shows the dimensions to construct the cupboard, which is basically the same as the 8-jar fermenter described earlier.

Cutting list

2 off $6' \times 15'' \times \frac{3}{4}''$ / 1m 829mm × 381mm × 19mm. Conti-board, blockboard, plywood. (Sides.)

6 off $22\frac{1}{2}'' \times 15'' \times \frac{3}{4}''$ / 572mm × 381mm × 19mm. Conti-board, blockboard, plywood. (Four shelves top & base.)

2 off $22\frac{1}{2}'' \times 6'' \times \frac{3}{4}''$ / 572mm × 152mm × 19mm. Contiboard, blockboard, plywood. (Shelves.)

1 off $15'' \times 3'' \times \frac{3}{4}''$ / 381mm × 76mm × 19mm. Contiboard, blockboard, plywood. (Division between drawers.)

2 off $6' \times 12'' \times \frac{3}{4}''$ / 1m 829mm × 305mm × 19mm. Conti-board, blockboard, plywood. (Doors.)

2 off $24'' \times 3'' \times 1\frac{1}{2}''$ / 610mm × 76mm × 38mm softwood. (Plinth, front and back.)

2 off $15'' \times 3'' \times 1\frac{1}{2}''$ / 381mm × 76mm × 38mm softwood. (Plinth, ends.)

1 off $6' \times 24'' \times \frac{1}{8}''$ / 1m 829mm × 610mm × 3mm hardboard. (Back.)

72 off $2'' \times \frac{1}{4}''$ / 51mm × 6mm hardwood dowels.

12 $1\frac{1}{2}''$ / 38mm × 8 gauge screws for screwing bottom shelf to plinth.

$1\frac{1}{2}''$ / 38mm and 2" / 51mm nails, 3 pairs 2" / 51mm hinges and screws, 4 cupboard catches, 2 handles to choice, $\frac{3}{4}''$ / 19mm pins and glue.

DRAWER TRAYS

4 off $10\frac{7}{8}'' \times 3'' \times \frac{3}{4}''$ / 276mm × 76mm × 19mm softwood. (Fronts and backs.)

4 off $13\frac{1}{2}'' \times 3'' \times \frac{3}{4}''$ / 343mm × 76mm × 19mm softwood. (Sides.)

2 off $10\frac{7}{8}'' \times 15'' \times \frac{1}{8}''$ / 276mm × 381mm × 3mm hardboard or plywood. (Bottom.)

$\frac{3}{4}''$ / 19mm hardboard or panel pins and $1\frac{1}{2}''$ / 38mm oval nails, glue.

Notes on assembly

The division between the drawers should be fixed in place with glue and $1\frac{1}{2}''$ ovals before the shelves are fitted to the sides.

The plinth should be mitred at the corners, glued nailed and assembled and fitted to the bottom of the cabinet before the back is fixed in place.

The front and back of the drawers are glued and nailed to the ends of the sides, the hardboard base is glued and pinned in place with the smooth side to the inside of the drawer. A $1''$ diameter hole is formed in the drawer fronts to provide a method of opening. Drawers usually need planing or sanding to make them fit.

Three hinges are used to hang each door and a catch is required at the top and the bottom.

The electrical layout is as shown in Fig. 18. The choice of finish is left to the constructor and is detailed in Chapter 1.

Tools required

Saw, hammer, nail punch, brace, drill bits, screwdriver, rule, trysquare, coping saw.

Record Card
Index Box

We have settled on standard $6'' \times 4''$ cards obtainable from most stationers for a few shillings per hundred for keeping our winemaking records, and we have constructed an index box to keep them tidy and readily available.

To make this box you will need two pieces plywood $7'' \times 5'' \times \frac{1}{4}''$ for the front and back, two pieces plywood $3\frac{1}{2}'' \times 5'' \times \frac{1}{4}''$ for the ends and two pieces for the top and bottom, $7'' \times 4'' \times \frac{1}{8}''$ thick.

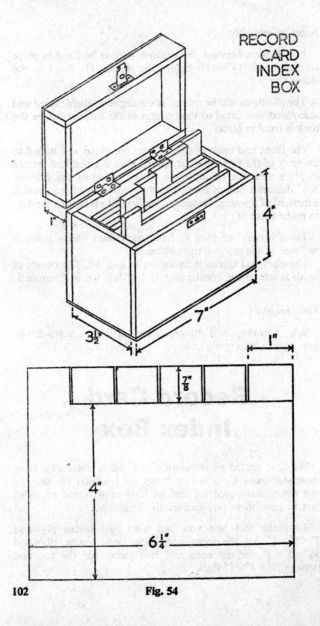

RECORD
CARD
INDEX
BOX

4"

7"

3½"

1"

7⁄8"

4"

6¼"

1"

Fig. 54

The ends are glued and pinned between the front and back pieces and the thinner pieces of plywood are glued and pinned on to form the box. When the glue has hardened, smooth all rough edges with glasspaper, then pencil a line around the box 1″ down from the top. With a fine toothed saw, cut the box in two along the pencil line to form the container and the lid. Glasspaper the sawn edges and fit two small trinket box hinges and a fastener.

The six interior divisions are cut from $\frac{1}{8}$″ plywood, hardboard or stiff cardboard, $6\frac{1}{4}$″ × 5″ with a tag left at staggered intervals along the top.

After painting, the tags on the interior division can be marked to allow you to locate a recipe easily.

Bottle Carrier

We have all experienced the difficulty of carrying armfuls of bottles to and from the store, etc., especially if the loft is used for storage. A simply made bottle carrier, similar to the ones that milkmen have been using for many years, but constructed of plywood, makes the transportation of bottles really easy.

Cutting list

1 off 13″ × 10$\frac{1}{2}$″ × $\frac{1}{4}$ / 330mm × 267mm × 6mm plywood. (Centre piece, cut to shape.)

2 off 7$\frac{3}{4}$″ × 4$\frac{3}{4}$″ × $\frac{1}{4}$″ / 197mm × 121mm × 6mm plywood. (Ends.)

2 off 10$\frac{1}{2}$″ × 4$\frac{3}{4}$″ × $\frac{1}{4}$″ / 267mm × 121mm × 6mm plywood. (Front and back.)

1 off 10$\frac{1}{2}$″ × 7$\frac{1}{4}$″ × $\frac{1}{4}$″ / 267mm × 184mm × 6mm plywood. (Base.)

8 off 4$\frac{1}{2}$″ × $\frac{1}{2}$″ / 114mm × 13mm quadrant or arris.

2 off 1$\frac{1}{2}$″ / 38mm squares of $\frac{1}{4}$″ / 6mm plywood, cut to a triangular shape. (Corner feet.)

BOTTLE CARRIER

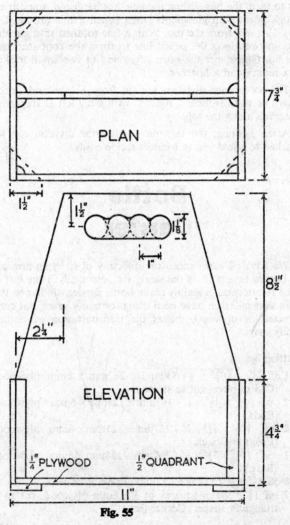

Fig. 55

Construction

Cut the centre piece to shape as shown in Fig. 55. Mark and cut out slot grip with a coping saw and clean up the rough edges. Glue and pin the centre piece to the middle of the base. The front, back and end pieces are fixed by the same method to the edge of the base. The quadrants are glued and pinned in position to give added strength. The $1\frac{1}{2}''$ squares are cut diagonally in half and one piece is fixed to each underside corner of the base to form the feet. Leave until the adhesive has set, rub down with coarse and fine glass paper and paint to choice as in Chapter 1.

Tools required

Handsaw, coping saw, hammer, rule, trysquare, punch, bradawl.

Malt Grain Crusher

This hand operated crusher can easily reduce malt grain to the desired size without scattering the particles all over the place.

Mark out the $\frac{1}{4}''$ plywood side pieces and cut two holes in each piece very slightly larger than the diameter of the rolling pin. (No exact size can be given as the old fashioned type wooden rolling pins often vary in diameter.) The holes should almost touch and it is usual for the wafer thin piece between the holes to break away. Although an adjuster is fitted later, care in setting out and cutting or boring the holes is very important.

Glue and pin the ends to the side pieces, ensuring that the holes are exactly opposite. While the glue is hardening, cut the rolling pin in half, draw a line around the circumference

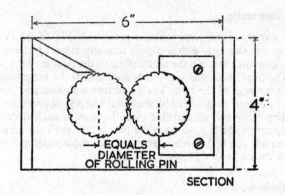

SECTION

MALT GRAIN
CRUSHER
fig.

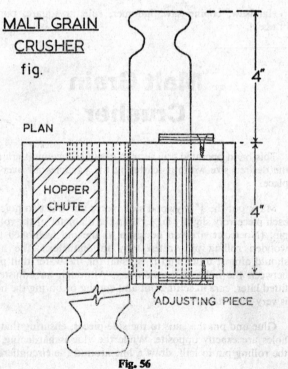

PLAN

Fig. 56

of each portion, 4in. from the cut end. With the corner of a sharp chisel, cut $\frac{1}{16}''$ deep grooves from the pencil line to the cut end and approximately $\frac{1}{4}''$ apart.

Cut the hopper chute pieces to fit, with the higher end bevelled on the underside to fit tight against the end pieces. Shape the lower end (Fig. 56), to direct the grain on to the rollers and glue and pin into position. Cut a hole the same diameter as the rolling pin in the centre of the adjusting piece and cut in half as shown. Place the rollers into the holes and fit the adjusting pieces to the outside of the sides. Set the rollers $\frac{1}{16}''$ apart and screw the adjusters to hold the rollers in position. Glass paper all rough edges.

BASE/COLLECTING BOX

Glue and pin the end pieces to the sides and fix base. Cut the inside bearers to size and glue and pin $\frac{1}{2}''$ down from the top edge. Glass paper all rough edges.

All surfaces, except the grooved part of the rollers and their bearing surfaces, may be coated with polyurethane.

To use, place the crusher in the collecting box and fill the hopper with grain. Grip the handle part of each roller and rotate the rollers in opposite directions to force the grain between them.

Cutting list

Crusher

2 off $6'' \times 4'' \times \frac{1}{2}''$ / 152mm × 102mm × 13mm ply. (Sides.)

2 off $4'' \times 4'' \times \frac{3}{8}''$ / 102mm × 102mm × 10mm ply. (Ends.)

2 off $3'' \times 2\frac{1}{4}'' \times \frac{1}{4}''$ / 76mm × 57mm × 6mm ply. (Hopper chute pieces.)

1 off $3'' \times 3\frac{1}{2}'' \times \frac{1}{4}''$ / 76mm × 89mm × 6mm ply. (Adjusting pieces.)

1 16″ / 406mm rolling pin approx. $1\frac{3}{4}''$ / 44mm diameter. Must be hardwood.

Base-Collecting box

2 off $6\frac{3}{4}'' \times 5'' \times \frac{3}{8}''$ / 171mm × 127mm × 10mm ply. (Sides.)

2 off $4\frac{3}{4}'' \times 5'' \times \frac{3}{8}''$ / 121mm × 127mm × 10mm ply. (Ends.)

1 off $7\frac{1}{2}'' \times 4\frac{3}{4}'' \times \frac{1}{8}''$ / 190mm × 121mm × 3mm ply or hardboard. (Base.)

2 off $6'' \times 1'' \times \frac{1}{2}''$ / 152mm × 25mm × 13mm softwood. (Inside bearers.)

1 off $4'' \times 1'' \times \frac{1}{2}''$ / 102mm × 25mm × 13mm softwood. (Inside bearers.

1″ / 25mm panel pins.

4 $\frac{5}{8}''$ / 16mm round head woodscrews.

Tools required

Tenon saw, coping or padsaw, chisels, brace and bit, hammer, rule, trysquare, bradawl, screwdriver, nail punch, plane.

Shelves and Shelving

To have enough shelves to store all those gallon jars is often the winemaker's dream. Described here are several methods of shelving to help your dream come true.

SUPPORTING SHELVES

There are a variety of ways to support shelves on a wall and the simple methods described are well within the scope of the average handyman. The strength of the shelf depends on the way the supports are fixed. It is essential that a suitable length of $1'' \times 2''$ softwood is properly plugged and screwed (see Chapter 1) vertically to the wall to take the metal angle shelf brackets, gallows brackets, or patent shelving uprights, whichever system is being used. A minimum height of 14″, for a gallon jar without an airlock, should be allowed between the shelves when determining the length of the vertical fixing batten.

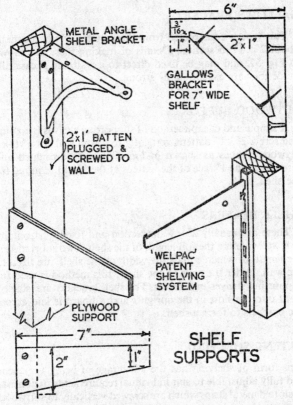

METAL ANGLE SHELF BRACKET

6"

$\frac{3}{16}$"

1"

2"×1"

GALLOWS BRACKET FOR 7" WIDE SHELF

2"×1" BATTEN PLUGGED & SCREWED TO WALL

'WELPAC' PATENT SHELVING SYSTEM

PLYWOOD SUPPORT

7"

2"

1"

SHELF SUPPORTS

Fig. 57

METAL ANGLE SHELF BRACKETS

These can be obtained from any hardware or Do-it-Yourself shop, in pressed steel, usually painted, cast alloy or wrought iron. The easiest way to fix the bracket is by screwing them to strips of 2″ × 1″ softwood, which are plugged and screwed vertically to the wall.

109

GALLOWS BRACKET

This type is constructed from three pieces of wood usually about $2'' \times 1''$ in section. Details of making these are shown in Fig. 57, and may be fixed direct to a wall and if carefully made they are exceptionally strong.

PLYWOOD SUPPORTS

A simple and cheap method of supporting shelves is to plug and screw $2'' \times 1''$ battens vertically to a wall and cut $\frac{1}{2}''$ thick plywood shapes as shown in Fig. 57, which are glued and screwed to the $1''$ face of the battens at the height required for the shelf.

SHELF BEARERS

These are usually $2'' \times \frac{3}{4}''$ in section and fixed horizontally to a wall running the full length of the shelf. Two short pieces, the length of which equals the width of the shelf, are fixed to the wall. under the ends of the shelf; this method is used for supporting shelves in a recess. The shelf brackets are shaped to fit into the slots in the uprights and a board is laid across the brackets to form a shelf.

PATENT SHELVING

This form of shelving has the advantage of being very neat and fully adjustable to suit individual requirements. It consists of slotted metal strips which are screwed vertically to softwood battens, plugged and screwed to the wall.

SHELVING

Suitable shelf sections for holding gallon jars would be $7''$ wide and $1''$ thick, cut from either softwood, hardwood, blockboard or plywood. The cheapest material would be softwood. Blockboard or plywood would require a strip of wood fixed to the front edge of the shelf to give a neat appearance. It is most important when using blockboard, that the core slats run the length of the shelf. $7'' \times 1''$ timber is adequate

SHELVES IN A RECESS

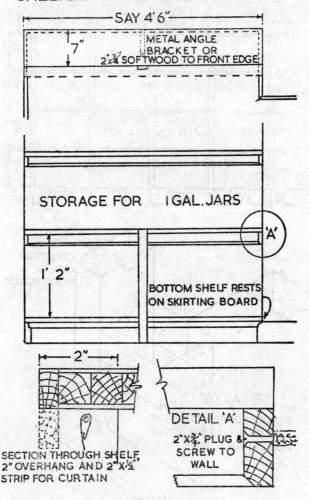

|←————— SAY 4' 6" —————→|

7"

METAL ANGLE
BRACKET OR
2" x 3/4" SOFTWOOD TO FRONT EDGE

STORAGE FOR   1 GAL. JARS

'A'

1' 2"

BOTTOM SHELF RESTS
ON SKIRTING BOARD

|← 2" →|

SECTION THROUGH SHELF,
2" OVERHANG AND 2" X 1/2"
STRIP FOR CURTAIN

DETAIL 'A'
2" X 3/4" PLUG &
SCREW TO
WALL

Fig. 58

SHELVES ON A STRAIGHT WALL

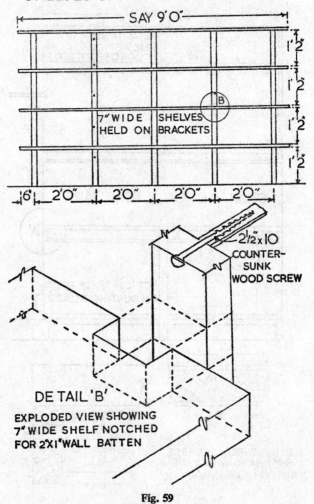

SAY 9'0"

1'2 1'2 1'2 1'2

7" WIDE SHELVES HELD ON BRACKETS

B

6" 2'0" 2'0" 2'0" 2'0"

2½ x 10 COUNTER-SUNK WOOD SCREW

DETAIL 'B'

EXPLODED VIEW SHOWING 7" WIDE SHELF NOTCHED FOR 2"X1" WALL BATTEN

Fig. 59

for holding gallon jars providing the shelf is continuous and the distance between the brackets is approximately 2 ft. This may seem close for the supports, but the full gallon jar weighs 16 lb. and this would mean that eight jars on a shelf 4′ 6″ long, supported by three brackets, would be carrying a weight of some 128 lb.

IN A RECESS

Many houses have a recess, for example the one adjacent to the chimney breast, that just asks to have shelves fitted into it. Fig. 58 shows the position to fix the shelf bearers on to the back and side walls. If a bank of three shelves were fitted in the living room, the top shelf could be 2 in. greater in depth than the lower ones and a piece of curtaining to match those in the room could be hung from the underside of the overhang. A 2″ × ½″ strip of hardwood glued to the front edge of the overhang would conceal the curtain wires and give a neat finish. For easy cleaning of the top shelf it may be covered with self adhesive or laminated plastic sheeting.

ON A STRAIGHT WALL

Any of the following methods of supporting shelves can be used; metal angle shelf brackets, gallows brackets, plywood supports, or patent shelving. Whichever method is selected they must not be fixed more than 2ft. apart. For example, a 4′ 6″ shelf length requires three supports, one mounted centrally and the others situated 3 in. in from the ends.

If one end of the shelf butts to a corner a short length of bearer can be plugged and screwed to the return wall in lieu of a shelf bracket.

CHAPTER 8

Young Winemaker

Children often like to help Dad with the work that he is doing (frequently to his annoyance). We have experienced this and find that giving them something they can make by themselves keeps them quiet—for a while!

By showing them how to make some of the items in this chapter, they can be kept occupied and at the same time produce useful articles, very often out of scrap materials. The only "tools" required are a tape measure, scissors, needle and thread, rule and a pot of glue. Covering the work surface with newspaper often makes clearing up easier!

"DAD'S APRON"

This novel apron always causes amusement and encourages the owner to wear it at party times. The sword and belt are cut from contrasting material and stitched by hand, or machine if available, on to the apron as shown in Fig. 60. It would be advisable to use a good quality linen for the apron and strings, with the embellishments cut from either linen or felt.

BEER MATS

These mats are not the true absorbent type, but do allow you to add a touch of individuality when serving drinks. They can be made to match curtains or wallpaper or can contrast, as desired. The basis of these mats is a disc of card between 3 and 4 in. in diameter. If covering with wallpaper 2 discs are required, one the same size as the cardboard base and the other about half an inch larger all round. Paste the cardboard base in the centre of the larger disc and make V cuts around the edge, about a quarter of an inch apart. Apply paste to the overhanging segments and fold over the cardboard rim to form a neat edge. The smaller disc is then pasted on

DAD'S APRON

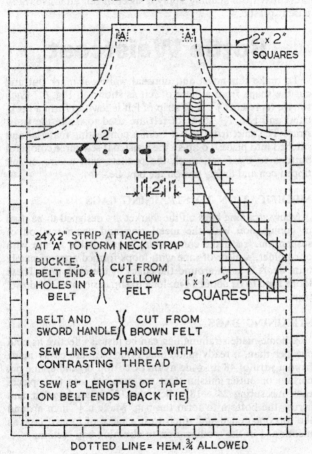

2" x 2" SQUARES

A   A

2"

1" 2" 1"

24" x 2" STRIP ATTACHED
AT 'A' TO FORM NECK STRAP

BUCKLE,
BELT END &   CUT FROM
HOLES IN   YELLOW
BELT   FELT

1" x 1"
SQUARES

BELT AND   CUT FROM
SWORD HANDLE BROWN FELT

SEW LINES ON HANDLE WITH
CONTRASTING THREAD

SEW 18" LENGTHS OF TAPE
ON BELT ENDS (BACK TIE)

DOTTED LINE = HEM. ¾" ALLOWED

Fig. 60

to cover the cuts. Washable papers obviously give the best results as they can easily be wiped clean. This method can be used when covering the cardboard with material, but to prevent it from staining apply a sheet of self adhesive transparent plastic.

Bottle Waistcoat

To make this novel and unusual waistcoat mark out and cut the shape from a piece of felt as shown in Fig. 61. Each square represents $\frac{1}{4}''$. A 6″ strip of felt is sewn to form a neckband and two $7\frac{1}{2}''$ strips of felt are used to make the waist strap. The shirt front is cut from a contrasting material and stitched into place. To finish the waistcoat sew three colourful buttons to the front, mark the pockets with a biro or felt tipped pen and finally sew on the bow tie.

MODIFICATION TO STRAINING BAGS

Many straining bags on the market are designed to be used in conjunction with the metal ring and chain method of suspension. To make commercial bags suitable to use with our holder, a piece of tape with loops formed approximately 6 in. apart is sewn around the edges of the open end. These loops need to be about $1\frac{1}{2}$ in. long to slip easily over the dowel pegs.

STRAINING BAGS

A home-made straining bag can be just as effective as, and cheaper than, a ready made one. Four bags are easily made from a yard of 48 in. wide nylon or cotton organdie, fine net curtain or butter muslin. Cut the material into four pieces each measuring 24″ × 18″. Sew the 18″ edges together and across the bottom to form the bag. Make a $\frac{1}{2}''$ hem around the top open edge and stitch to it a piece of looped tape as mentioned in the modification to straining bag section.

PRESS BAGS

Pulp should never be tipped into a press without its being contained in some sort of bag. A bag can be made from a piece of material, 36″ × 18″ to suit the presses described in the second chapter of this book (this size bag can be used in the majority of presses up to two gallons capacity). Simply sew the short edges and the bottom edges together and form a ½″ hem around the top. The materials recommended for the straining bags can be used for making press bags.

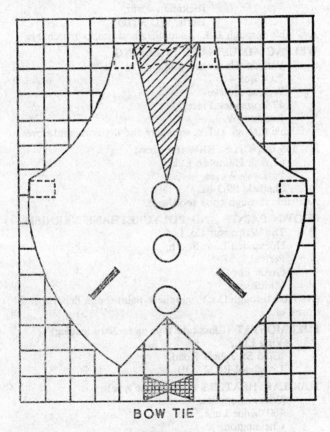

BOW TIE

Fig. 61

Appendix

CONTIBOARD
>Trade name of Aaronson Brothers Ltd.,
>Timber Products Division,
>Church Wharf,
>Rickmansworth,
>Herts. WD 3 IJD

Available through D.I.Y. suppliers and timber merchants.

WELPAC ADJUSTABLE SHELVING
>Welpac (Hardware) Ltd.,
>P.O. Box 44,
>Welpac House,
>47 Brunswick Place,
>London, W. 1.

Available through D.I.Y. suppliers and departmental stores.

No. 165 BENCH SCREW (for press)
>C. & J. Hampton Ltd.,
>Parkway Works,
>Sheffield S9 3 BL

Available through good toolshops.

CROWN PAINTS AND POLYURETHANE VARNISH
>The Walpamur Co. Ltd.,
>Horsenden Lane South,
>Perival,
>Green Ford,
>Middlesex.

Available through D.I.Y. suppliers, paint shops, departmental stores, etc.

THERMOSTAT (Glass tube type up to 300w loading)
>Vina Ltd.,
>63/65 St. John's Road,
>Liverpool RS22 9QB

TUBULAR HEATERS (Greenhouse type)
>Winery Supplies,
>160 Moor Lane,
>Chessington,
>Surrey.

Metric Equivalents

TEMPERATURE

Degrees Fahrenheit to Centigrade										
C	**0**	**1**	**2**	**3**	**4**	**5**	**6**	**7**	**8**	**9**
0	32	34	36	37	39	41	43	45	46	48
10	50	52	54	55	57	59	61	63	64	66
20	68	70	72	73	75	77	79	81	82	84
30	86	88	90	91	93	95	97	99	100	102
40	104	106	108	109	111	113	115	117	118	120
50	122	124	126	127	129	131	133	135	136	138
60	140	142	144	145	147	149	151	153	154	156
70	158	160	162	163	165	167	169	171	172	174
80	176	178	180	181	183	185	187	189	190	192
90	194	196	198	199	201	203	205	207	208	210
100	212	214	216	217	219	221	223	225	226	228

LINEAL MEASURE

Inches to Millimetres

Millimetres	0	1	2	3	4	5	6	7	8	9
0	0	1/32	3/32	1/8	5/32	3/16	1/4	9/32	5/16	11/32
10	13/32	7/16	15/32	1/2	9/16	19/32	5/8	21/32	23/32	3/4
20	25/32	13/16	7/8	29/32	15/16	1	1 1/32	1 1/16	1 3/32	1 5/32
30	1 3/16	1 7/32	1 1/4	1 5/16	1 11/32	1 3/8	1 13/32	1 15/32	1 1/2	1 17/32
40	1 9/16	1 5/8	1 21/32	1 11/16	1 23/32	1 25/32	1 13/16	1 27/32	1 7/8	1 15/16
50	1 31/32	2	2 1/16	2 3/32	2 1/8	2 5/32	2 7/32	2 1/4	2 9/32	2 5/16
60	2 3/8	2 13/32	2 7/16	2 15/32	2 17/32	2 9/16	2 19/32	2 5/8	2 11/16	2 23/32
70	2 3/4	2 25/32	2 27/32	2 7/8	2 29/32	2 15/16	3	3 1/32	3 1/16	3 1/8
80	3 5/32	3 3/16	3 7/32	3 9/32	3 5/16	3 11/32	3 3/8	3 7/16	3 15/32	3 1/2
90	3 17/32	3 19/32	3 5/8	3 21/32	3 11/16	3 3/4	3 25/32	3 13/16	3 27/32	3 29/32
100	3 15/16	3 31/32	4 1/32	4 1/16	4 3/32	4 1/8	4 3/16	4 7/32	4 1/4	4 9/32
200	7 7/8	7 29/32	7 15/16	8	8 1/32	8 1/16	8 1/8	8 5/32	8 3/16	8 7/32
300	11 13/16	11 27/32	11 7/8	11 15/16	11 31/32	12	12 1/16	12 3/32	12 1/8	12 5/32

Other AW Books

C. J. J. Berry
FIRST STEPS IN WINEMAKING

—the acknowledged introduction to the subject; acclaimed by thousands (over 1 million have already been sold). Unbeatable at the price; winemaking clearly explained, over 150 reliable recipes, using the hydrometer; mead; cider; perry; judging; exhibiting. Illustrated.

J. R. Mitchell, L.I.R.C., A.I.F.S.T.
SCIENTIFIC WINEMAKING—MADE EASY

—this is at once the most advanced and most practical textbook on the subject so far, written by a scientist who is a quality control executive employed by a group of companies owning some of Britain's largest wine interests. A glance at the chapter headings shows its scope: The way it should start (sterilisation) etc.); Selecting the right equipment; Extracting and adjusting fruit juices for fermentation; Preparing the yeast starter; Managing the fermentation; Racking, sweetening and fortifying; aging; Filtration and finings; Bottling; Storing and serving; How to evolve recipes; Tasting and glossary of terms; Micro-organisms of fermentation and spoilage; Troubles and cures; Simplified wine chemistry; and useful test procedures. Packed with new information. Fully illustrated, 260 pages. The book any serious winemaker must have.

Tilly Timbrell and Bryan Acton
THE WINEMAKER'S COOKBOOK

—this brilliant new book will really make your mouth water! The only one available on this subject, it gives you a whole range of exciting *hors d'oeuvres*, soups, fish, meat, poultry and dessert dishes that can be made using your own home-made wines. *The Winemaker's Cookbook* is essentially practical cookery, demanding no rare and expensive ingredients, all its recipes have been tested and approved by a team of cooks and tasters!

Dr. F. W. Beech and Dr. A. Pollard
WINEMAKING AND BREWING

—this authoritative new book by these two experts from the Long Ashton Research Station covers the theory and practice of winemaking and brewing in detail; how to grow grapes, how to make wines, perries, ciders, ales, punches, beers, fruit juices and vinegars and how to judge.

Gillian Pearkes
GROWING GRAPES IN BRITAIN

—a handbook for winemakers. Written specially for the English viticulturist, it tells the history of vinegrowing in England, explains that it *is* possible to grow and ripen wine grapes outdoors, and covers fully choice of site and varieties, planting, training, manuring, pruning, pest control, propagation, harvesting and winemaking. The most detailed book available on this subject, and indispensable whether you have six vines or six thousand.

Edited by C. J. J. Berry
"AMATEUR WINEMAKER" RECIPES

—this useful AW paperback contains a fascinatingly varied collection of over 200 recipes garnered from several years' issues of the winemaker's favourite magazine. They include many by that well-known Birmingham winemaker Cyril Shave, a specialist in wines from herbs, and a particularly useful set of recipes for liqueurs, punches mulls, fruit cups and other party drinks. The cartoons are by Rex Royle.

C. J. J. Berry
WINEMAKING WITH CANNED AND DRIED FRUIT

—the simplest, most convenient and most economical of all. How to make delightful wines from the ready-prepared ingredients you can find at your grocers or supermarket, tinned fruits and juices, pulps, purées, pie fillings, concentrates, jams, jellies and dried fruit.

C. J. J. Berry
130 NEW WINEMAKING RECIPES

—the companion paperback to *First Steps*, augmenting its 150 recipes with 130 others using newly available ingredients. Together these two books give you a unique collection of up-to-date recipes. It is also a complete instruction book in itself. Illustrations, and 50 amusing cartoons by Rex Royle.

Bryan Acton and Peter Duncan
MAKING WINES LIKE THOSE YOU BUY

—how to make your own Sherry, Port, Madeira, Champagne, Chianti, red and white table and dessert wines, hocks, Moselles, etc. A fascinating chapter tells how to make a whole range of aperitifs (Vermouth, etc.) and liqueurs and all this at a fraction of what they would cost to buy. The book for the really progressive winemaker. 76 recipes for wines, 56 for liqueurs. Fully illustrated.

P. Duncan and B. Acton
PROGRESSIVE WINEMAKING
—this magnificent, fact-packed volume by these two well-known winemaking experts has been hailed as one of the best books of the decade; it deals with advanced winemaking in a readable way, and carries its erudition lightly. This really fat volume—500 pages —is really two books in one. Part I deals with the scientific theory of winemaking, sulphite, acidity, tannin, water, the hydrometer, the meaning of pH, yeast, nutrients, preparation of the must, fermentation, racking, clarification, continuous filtering, building a press, blending, fortification, wine disorders, etc. Part II deals with the production of quality wines, both red and white, and the making of Sherry, Port and Madeira type wines, and sparkling wines—all in the greatest detail. Fully illustrated.

C. J. J. Berry
HOME BREWED BEERS AND STOUTS
—the very first full-length book on this fascinating subject to be published, and still the best; many thousands of copies have been sold. Bang up-to-date, it covers: The story of ale and beer; Types of beer and stout; Background to brewing; Brewing at home from barley, malt, malt extract, dried malt extract, other herbs and grits; How to make lager, pale ale, light, mild, brown, bitter stout, barley wine, mock beers. Well illustrated.

Ken Shales
BREWING BETTER BEERS
—a lively paperback on home brewing: by a real master of the craft, Ken Shales, of Basildon (which is likely to be renamed Boozledon from now on, it seems!) This book gives Ken's personal, well-tried recipes for all types of malt liquor from lightest lager to blackest double-stout and explains many finer points of brewing technique. A book no really thirsty home brewer should be without!

C. J. J. Berry
HINTS ON HOME BREWING
—a concise and well-illustrated "rapid course" for home brewers, containing all the basic, down-to-earth essentials.

Dean Jones
HOME BREWING SIMPLIFIED
—detailed recipes for ten types of bottled and draught beer; hints, tips and know how. Clear, easy-to-follow directions for successful brewing.

JUDGING HOME-MADE WINES

—the official detailed handbook published by the National Guild of Judges. Essential for all would-be judges and stewards. Full procedure; specimen schedules for all sizes of show; specimen show rules; constitution of Guild; how to qualify as a National Judge

T. Edwin Belt
PRESERVING WINEMAKING INGREDIENTS

—a useful AW book, and the only one available dealing with this aspect of winemaking. It tells how, in times of plenty or surplus, to preserve fruit, flowers and vegetables for use later in the year, when time and utensils are available. It deals in detail with preservation by means of drying (how to dry, for instance, rose hips, elderberries, sloes, bilberries, apples, etc.), chemical preservation, deep freezing, and chunk bottling. Also how to make syrups, jams and jellies from wild and garden fruit.

Bryan Acton and Peter Duncan
MAKING MEAD

—the up-to-date approach to man's most ancient drink. How to make meads (sweet and dry), melomels, hyppocras, metheglin, pyments, cyser, etc. The only full-length paperback on this winemaking speciality available.

PROGRAMME IDEAS

—the AW's printed list to help programme secretaries and others; how to construct a year's Circle programme; where to obtain speakers (on winemaking, brewing, commercial wines and allied subjects) films, coloured slides, social events and ideas, suggestions for outings, wine competitions, lists of judges, etc.

Cedric Austin
WHYS AND WHEREFORES OF WINEMAKING

—this book is outside the usual run of wine manuals. Its primary aim is to produce *better* wine by assisting the wine maker to *understand what he is doing*. For that reason, it is an essential handbook for use at any stage. Here are the pros and cons of different methods set out; the facts and fallacies separated; the function of ingredients and additives explained; the queries and indecisions cleared up. It will help beginners who wonder why recipes vary in ingredient and method to make the same wine, as well as experienced winemakers who, as their skill increases, wish to know why as well as how. The whys and wherefores of winemaking, expressed in a cheerful and readable style, are brought together in six sections, with an index to aid easy reference.